Bonner Studien zum globalen Wandel

Bonner Studien zum globalen Wandel

Herausgegeben von
Wolfram Hilz

Band 2

Kathrin Kästle

African Justice for African Healing

Justice, Reconciliation and Traditional Approaches in Rwanda

Tectum Verlag

Kathrin Kästle

African Justice for African Healing.
Justice, Reconciliation and Traditional Approaches in Rwanda

Bonner Studien zum globalen Wandel
Herausgegeben von Wolfram Hilz
Band 2

ISBN: 978-3-8288-2108-8
Umschlagabbildung: www.istockphoto.com, jordanchez

Besuchen Sie uns im Internet
www.tectum-verlag.de

Bibliografische Informationen der Deutschen Nationalbibliothek
Die Deutsche Nationalbibliothek verzeichnet diese Publikation in der Deutschen Nationalbibliografie; detaillierte bibliografische Angaben sind im Internet über http://dnb.ddb.de abrufbar.

This thesis is for Remy who has lost everything, and is still able to smile.

And for my parents who have always supported my dreams.

Vorwort des Herausgebers

Der Konflikt in Ruanda mit dem Genozid des Jahres 1994 und rund 1 Million Toten gilt unter den ethno-politischen Konflikten der 1990er Jahre als trauriger Höhepunkt. In der wissenschaftlichen Auseinandersetzung mit diesem Konflikt bilden sowohl die Abläufe während des Genozids, als auch das eklatante Versagen der internationalen Staatengemeinschaft bei der Verhinderung der Gewaltexzesse sowie des wirksamen Einsatzes von internationalen Truppen den Schwerpunkt. Das sog. Post-Conflict-Peace-Building mit den Aspekten der innergesellschaftlichen und justiziellen Aufarbeitung stellen dagegen noch Randbereich der politikwissenschaftlichen Forschung dar. Dies liegt nicht zuletzt daran, dass Prozesse der Aussöhnung nach derartigen Gräueltaten in jedem Fall höchst unterschiedlich ablaufen.

Kathrin Kästle liefert mit ihrer Studie „African Justice for African Healing – Justice, reconciliation and traditional approaches in Ruanda" an der Schnittstelle zwischen rechts- und sozialwissenschaftlicher Forschung völlig neue Einblicke in das Spannungsfeld zwischen gerichtlicher Aufarbeitung von Verbrechen nach westlichen Vorstellungen und Ansätzen zur Versöhnung durch traditionelle Instrumente. Hierbei weist sie auch darauf hin, dass es nicht zuletzt von der rechten Balance zwischen Gerechtigkeit und Aussöhnung abhängt, ob ein erneuter Konfliktausbruch vermieden werden kann.
Die vorliegende Untersuchung in der Reihe „Bonner Studien zum globalen Wandel" liefert somit Hinweise auf die Neuartigkeit der internationalen Herausforderungen, die durch inter-ethnische Spannungen entstehen. Dies betrifft im Falle Ruandas sowohl den Aspekt der rechtzeitigen und ausreichenden Reaktion der internationalen Staatengemeinschaft angesichts einer drohen Katastrophe als auch die Facette der erforderlichen Konfliktnachsorge als Präventionsinstrument.

Prof. Dr. Wolfram Hilz

Table of Contents

1 Introduction

1.1 Context

Between 500.000 and one million people lost their lives in Rwanda in 1994 in what has become known as the swiftest genocide in human history. It lasted 100 days and an estimated 5.5 persons were killed every minute, leaving Rwanda with a tenth of its population dead. The victims belonged mainly to the minority Tutsi ethnic group, but moderate Hutu and their families were also killed by militia, army elements and ordinary citizens.[1]

The genocide was the final violent explosion of ethnic tensions that had built up for decades. Rwanda had become a part of the German East Africa colony in 1899. After the First World War, Belgium took over and reigned Rwanda and neighbouring Burundi under a League of Nations (and later United Nations) mandate. The Belgians used the Tutsi aristocracy in Rwanda to govern the territory through indirect rule, transforming the majority Hutu population into second class citizens. On the eve of independence in 1959 the Belgians shifted their allegiance to the Hutu, however, as the Tutsi intellectuals demanded an end to colonization all too self-confidently. With the help of the colonizers the Hutu were able to organize what has become known as the Hutu revolution and gained power. For the first time in Rwanda's history systematic violence between the groups occurred and many Tutsi left the country fleeing the massacres.[2]

In 1962, Rwanda became independent and was governed by the Hutu president Gregoire Kayibanda. Massacres against Tutsi continued to occur and were fuelled by attempts on behalf of the Tutsi exiles to force their way back into the country and take power again. In 1972 the Tutsi minority government and army massacred large parts of the Hutu population in Burundi. These massacres are today regarded as the first genocide in the region. The events in Burundi immediately sparked new violence against the Tutsi in Rwanda and led to a second wave of Rwandan Tutsi refugees to the neighbouring states. In 1973 Major General Juvenal Habyarimana seized power in a bloodless coup

---

1 See Jackson Nyamuya Maogoto: The International Criminal Tribunal for Rwanda. A Distorting Mirror. Casting Doubt on its Actor Oriented Approach in Addressing the Rwandan Genocide, in: African Journal on Conflict Resolution, Vol. 3 (2003) 1, in: http://www.accord.org.za/ajcr/2003-1/accordr_v3_n1_a8.pdf (16.12.2007), pp. 65f.

2 See Thomas Scheen: Der Kongo und Ruanda. Konflikte in der Region der Großen Seen, Bonn 2004 (FES Analyse), in: http://library.fes.de/pdf-files/id/02121.pdf (16.12.2007), pp. 4ff.

d'état. His party "Mouvement Revolutionaire Nationale pour le Developpement" (MRND) was instituted as the only party in Rwanda. Despite Habyarimana's autocratic rule and the discrimination against the Tutsi minority the outbursts of violence became less frequent during the so-called second republic which lasted from 1973 until 1994.[3] Rwanda under Habyarimana was the darling of the donor community with low corruption rates and remarkable stability.[4] But rapid population growth and the lack of land led to growing tensions within Rwandan society from 1980 onwards.[5]

At the same time armed guerrilla movements from the diaspora started to attack Rwanda to enforce a return for the Tutsi refugees. These rebel groups were mainly made up of the children of the 1959 refugees that had grown up in refugee camps in Uganda and other neighbouring states. In 1990 the "Rwandan Patriotic Front" (RPF) under Paul Kagame invaded Northern Rwanda from their bases in Uganda. The Rwandan government troops were able to force the intruders back with the help of French troops that jumped to the rescue of their long time ally.[6] A civil war followed from 1990 until 1994 between the RPF and Rwandan government troops. In 1992 both parties started ceasefire negotiations in Arusha, Tanzania, and signed a peace treaty, known as the Arusha records, on the 4th of August 1993.[7] The United Nations (UN) sent a peacekeeping force to Rwanda to observe the peace process.[8] On the 6th of April 1994 the plane of president Habyarimana was shot down on its arrival at Kigali airport. The assassination of Habyarimana triggered the carefully planned genocide against moderate Hutu politicians and the Tutsi

3 See Jon Lunn: The African Great Lakes Region. An End to Conflict?, London 2006 (House of Commons Library Research Paper 06/51), in: http://www.parliament.uk/commons/lib/research/rp2006/rp06-051.pdf (16.12.2007), p. 37.

4 See Barbara Oomen: Donor-Driven Justice and its Discontents. The Case of Rwanda, in: Development and Change, Vol. 36 (2005) 5, p. 894.

5 See Günther Bächler: Violence Through Environmental Discrimination, Dordrecht et al. 1999 (Social Indicators Research Series Volume 2), p. 139.

6 See Gregory Mthembu-Salter: Mediation and Genocide in Rwanda and Burundi's Peace Agreement Without Peace, in: Track Two, Vol. 11 (2002) 5/6, in: http://ccrweb.ccr.uct.ac.za/archive/two/11_56/rwanda_chapter2.html (29.06.2008), [Paragraph 10].

7 See Gérard Prunier: The Rwanda Crisis 1959-1994. History of a Genocide, London 1995, p. 191. For a detailed analysis of the war, the peace talks and the democratization process see chapters 3-5.

8 See Roméo Dallaire: Shake Hands With the Devil. The Failure of Humanity in Rwanda, London 2004, p. 43. In this personal account of the peacekeeping exercise in Rwanda the Canadian commander of the blue berets gives an excellent insight into the failure of the UN intervention which was unable to stop the genocide.

population. The civil war broke out again.[9] The RPF launched a new offensive and conquered Kigali in July 1994. The extremist Rwandan government and the militias fled to the Kivu province in the east of the Democratic Republic of Congo (DRC), aided by the establishment of a humanitarian protection zone called "Zone Turquoise"[10] by the French. They took at least one million terrified Hutu refugees with them that feared the revenge of the Tutsi RPF.[11]
The RPF installed a new government in Kigali in compliance with the Arusha records and started to hunt down the remnants of the old regime in the DRC. In the meantime two million people inhabited the large UN refugee camps in the Kivu region of the DRC. "The Rwandan Patriotic Army" (RPA) – the successor of the RPF army – aimed at forcing these refugees back into Rwanda.[12] After the violent dissolution of the camps by the RPA most of the refugees returned to Rwanda in 1996. The militias and elements of the former Rwandan army fled deeper into the forests of the DRC to continue fighting the new regime in Kigali from beyond the border. More than 200.000 refugees have been "missing" since.[13]
The new government under President Pasteur Bizimungu – a Hutu member of the RPF – started to rebuild the totally destroyed country and bring the perpetrators of the genocide to justice. Rwanda was a country in shambles, with its infrastructure destroyed, its intellectuals killed and diseases like the Human Immunodeficiency Virus (HIV) and cholera ravaging the population.[14] The international community, which had failed to stop the genocide[15], now erected a tribunal for the prosecution of the masterminds orchestrating

---

9 See Alison Des Forges: Kein Zeuge darf überleben. Der Genozid in Ruanda, Hamburg 2002, p. 226.

10 The French had erected the humanitarian rescue zone as part of their „Operation Turquoise", approved by the Security Council of the UN. It saved the lives of many Tutsi during the last days of the genocide but also aided the flight of the perpetrators. The assessment of this intervention is highly disputed. See Philippe Guillot/Larry Minear: Soldiers to the Rescue. Humanitarian Lessons from Rwanda, Paris 1996.

11 See Scheen: Der Kongo und Ruanda, pp. 8f.

12 See Peter Molt: Eine gewaltsame "Lösung" der Flüchtlingsfrage, in: FAZ (02.11.1996), p. 8.

13 See Kisangani N. F. Emizet: The Massacre of Refugees in Congo. A Case of UN Peacekeeping Failure and International Law, in: Journal of Modern African Studies, Vol. 28 (2000) 2, p. 178.

14 See Oomen: Donor-Driven Justice, p. 900.

15 See Stefan Trines: Unterlassene Hilfeleistung bei Völkermord? Die UN und der Ruanda-Konflikt, in: Harding, Leonard (ed.): Ruanda – der Weg zum Völkermord. Vorgeschichte, Verlauf, Deutung, Hamburg 1998, p. 165.

the massacres, situated in Arusha, Tanzania.[16] In the years after the RPF victory ended the genocide, remnants of the extremist former regime continued to infiltrate the north and west of Rwanda to destabilize the new RPF-led government, killing genocide survivors and other civilians.[17] The RPF on the other hand launched the first Congo war by invading its neighbour several times to mete out the Hutu extremists once and for all. As this did not prove successful and the insurrections continued, Rwanda and its allies started the second Congo war in 1998 to oust the new president of the Congo, Laurent Kabila. Kabila in turn started to support the Rwandan extremists in their struggle to return to Rwanda by force.[18]

In Rwandan domestic policy the RPF – consisting mainly of Tutsi – as the leading force of the government began to tighten control of the society. Civil and political rights as well as the press were restricted in reaction to the outside threats. The government troops engaged frequently in human rights abuses and opposition politicians started to flee into exile.[19] Paul Kagame, the successful rebel leader of the RPF, became president in 2003.[20]

"Freedom House" ranked Rwanda in 2007 as a "not free" state, with further decline in political liberties since the previous year.[21] The Bertelsmann Transformation Index also acknowledges the ongoing drift towards an authoritarian dictatorship: Rwanda scores only on 103rd rank of 125 states on the democracy spectre.[22] The Human Development Index ranks Rwanda as 161st of 177

---

16 See UN Security Council: Security Council Resolution 955 8th November 1994, in: http://daccessdds.un.org/doc/UNDOC/GEN/N95/140/97/PDF/N9514097.pdf?OpenElement (16.12.2007).

17 See Andreas Wagner: Mauern des Schweigens brechen. Gegenseitiges Verständnis fördert den ruandischen Versöhnungsprozess, in: DED Brief, Vol. 44 (2007) 4, p. 28.

18 See International Crisis Group: Rwanda at the End of the Transition. A Necessary Political Liberalisation, Nairobi/Brüssel 2002 (International Crisis Group Africa Report No 53), in: http://www.crisisgroup.org/library/documents/report_archive/A400817_13112002.pdf (02.01.2008), p. 2. A good detailed analysis of the complicated regional scenario and the different key players can be found in the already cited text by Thomas Scheen.

19 See Helmut Strizek: Zur Lage der Menschenrechte in Ruanda. Leben nach dem Völkermord, Aachen 2003, p. 35.

20 See Rolf Hofmeier: Soziokulturelle Kurzanalyse Ruanda, Hamburg 2005, p. 15.

21 See Freedom House: Freedom House Index. Rwanda 2007, Washington/New York 2007, in: http://www.freedomhouse.org/template.cfm?page=22&year=2007&country=7259 (30.06.2008).

22 See Bertelsmann Stiftung: Bertelsmann Transformation Index 2008. Rwanda Country Report, Gütersloh 2008, in: http://www.bertelsmann-transformation-

countries. Almost all indicators show Rwanda to be in the last quarter of the statistic. It is assumed to fare even worse than the rest of Sub-Saharan Africa in the future. The Human Poverty Index ranks Rwanda on place 31 and almost half of the population is expected to not survive the age of 40.[23] Under these unpromising political and economic conditions the launch of the traditional Gacaca jurisdictions as a new measure to prosecute the lower-level perpetrators of the genocide by the government occurred in 2004.[24]
The political and historical context as well as the severe poverty influence the situation in Rwanda today profoundly and need to be kept in mind when analyzing the current events. It provides the background for Rwanda's quest for reconciliation and an assessment of the potential to reach this goal. In Rwanda, the largest government driven reconciliation process worldwide is taking place at present.[25] Dealing with the past and the consequences of violent conflict is an exceptionally difficult task in the land of the thousand hills, as never before a conflict claimed more victims in such a short time span, and never before so many ordinary citizens were involved in the killing.[26] Consequently the society is extremely divided and clearly split into opposing groups that are extremely suspicious of each other. The social fabric of Rwanda ceased to exist after the genocide.[27] Nevertheless victims and perpetrators are

---

index.de/fileadmin/pdf/Gutachten_BTI_2008/ESA/Rwanda.pdf (30.06.2008), p. 1.

23 See UNDP: Human Development Index. Going Beyond Income. Rwanda, New York 2007, in: http://hdrstats.undp.org/countries/country_fact_sheets/cty_fs_RWA.html (30.06.2008).

24 See Rwanda. Traditional Courts inaugurated, in: IRIN News (24.06.2004), in: http://www.irinnews.org/report.aspx?reportid=50380 (30.06.2008).
The Gacaca jurisdictions will be dealt with in detail in chapter 5 and are therefore only mentioned briefly here, despite their prominent status in the analysis of reconciliation in Rwanda.

25 Karen Brounéus: Reconciliation. Theory and Practice for Development Cooperation, Stockholm 2003 (SIDA), p. 11.

26 See Wolfgang Reinhardt: Signs of Hope after the Genocide. Healing and Reconciliation in Rwanda Today, in: Jörg Calliess (ed.): Zehn Jahre danach. Völkermord in Ruanda, Loccum 2005 (Dokumentation , despite their prominent status in the analysis of reconciliation in Rwanda.

26 Karen Brounéus: Reconciliation. Theory and Practice for Development Cooperation, Stockholm 2003 (SIDA), p. 11.

26 See Wolfgang Reinhardt: Signs of Hope after the Genocide. Healing and Reconciliation in Rwanda Today, in: Jörg Calliess (ed.): Zehn Jahre danach. Völkermord in Ruanda, Loccum 2005 (Dokumentation einer Tagung der evangelischen Akademie Loccum vom 5. bis 7. März 2004), pp. 187.

27 See Cyprian F. Fisiy: Of Journeys and Border Crossings. Return of Refugees, Identity, and Reconstruction in Rwanda, in: African Studies Review, Vol. 41 (1998) 1, pp. 23.

forced to coexist in the same state and thus need to find a way to deal with the past.

1.2 Aims and objectives

Research about Rwanda tends to concentrate on the genocide, its genesis and the conflict scenario in the great lakes in general while neglecting the post-war period and the quest for reconciliation.[28] This paper aims at filling this gap and examining the reconciliation process in Rwanda. The underlying assumption of the research question is that reconciliation is crucial for future peace and a successful dealing with the past. Personal experiences in Rwanda in 2007 have led to the author's opinion that reconciliation should be the focus of post-war politics in the country, as the failure of the process would have a grave negative effect on the ability to sustain a peaceful society.

Reconciliation is a vague concept and its success is difficult to evaluate.[29] However, a successful judicial process that establishes responsibility for past crimes and brings the offenders to justice is crucial to deal with the past and initiate a complex reconciliation process. This reconciliation process in turn is a safeguard against repeated violence and instability.[30] Therefore judicial approaches to deal with the genocide and their contribution to reconciliation are deemed as an appropriate focus point of this thesis. They are not only an important part of the reconciliation process but also easier to evaluate than other measures aiming at reconciliation.

The main objective is therefore: In what way do different judicial strategies on the international, national and local level – namely the International Criminal Tribunal for Rwanda (ICTR), the national courts and the Gacaca jurisdictions – contribute to reconciliation within Rwanda? Can dealing with the past through courts enhance reconciliation or will it rather achieve the opposite? A special emphasis will be placed on the contribution of the Gacaca jurisdictions to reconciliation in Rwanda. This form of local justice is the newest and seemingly most promising approach to date and will therefore be examined in greater detail than the national and international approaches to validate this assumption. This thesis aims at clarifying the question whether local Gacaca

---

28 See Eugenia Zorbas: Reconciliation in Post-genocide Rwanda, in: African Journal of Legal Studies, Vol. 1 (2004) 1, p. 47.

29 See Donna Pankhurst: Issues of Justice and Reconciliation in Complex Political Emergencies. Conceptualising Reconciliation, Justice and Peace, in: Third World Quarterly, Vol. 20 (1999) 1, p. 239.

30 See Sandrine Schilling: Gegen das Vergessen. Justiz, Wahrheitsfindung und Versöhnung nach dem Genozid in Ruanda durch Mechanismen traditioneller Justiz. Gacaca Gerichte, Frankfurt am Main 2005, p. 115.

jurisdictions are better suited to reconcile Rwandans than conventional approaches.
The judicial strategies in dealing with the genocide need to be analyzed in the context of current Rwandan politics as described above. The nature of the Rwandan regime to date is assumed to have an important impact on reconciliation and justice and therefore needs to be taken into account. If democracy is the best form of government to achieve reconciliation, as renowned conflict studies scholar David Bloomfield assumes[31], the authoritarian character of the current Rwandan regime is likely to have profound implications for reconciliation. The thesis will examine to what extent the political circumstances influence the reconciliation process in the context of judicial strategies and how politics and ethnicity relate to each other in contemporary Rwanda.

1.3 Research Methodology

The following study is based on essential primary sources as well as various books, article editions and magazine articles on reconciliation, conflict management, ethnicity, political transition and transitional justice in general as well as on the Rwandan crisis, history and politics in particular. It aims at extracting relevant contents and applying them to the Rwandan context, comparing different views on the topic to reach an overall assessment of justice and reconciliation in Rwanda.
The theoretical framework of reconciliation is analyzed in chapter 2. Important aspects of reconciliation such as restoration of relationships, acknowledgement of the past, change in attitudes, healing, forgiveness, truth and justice are defined and conceptualized in the Rwandan context. The thesis is mainly interested in the community level of reconciliation. Individual restoration of relationships and their importance for a reconciled society are explained as a basis for more general processes in the political sphere. Justice as an important tool to achieve reconciliation is discussed in an additional subsection, as it is the focus point of this thesis. Truth as an important ingredient of justice is also analyzed in detail, as well as forgiveness, which is the desired outcome of the justice process. The developed framework will then be used to examine reconciliation in Rwanda. It will be analyzed how the revealing of truth, acknowledgement by perpetrators and punishment contribute to restored relationships and a change in attitude.

---

31 See David Bloomfield: Reconciliation. An Introduction, in: David Bloomfield/Teresa Barnes/Luc Huyse (eds.): Reconciliation After Violent Conflict. A Handbook, Stockholm 2003 (IDEA), in: http://www.idea.int/publications/reconciliation/upload/reconciliation_full.pdf (12.01.2008), p. 10.

To fully understand what needs to be reconciled in Rwanda and which actors play important roles in the process, the genesis of the Rwandan conflict must be traced back. Chapter 3 does not aim at giving a complete account of Rwanda's history but rather concentrates on the interpretation of that history by the different ethnic groups. It outlines the making of ethnicity from precolonial times until the genocide in 1994 and clarifies the impact of that genocide on perceptions of ethnicity of both victims and perpetrators thereafter. The question whether Hutu and Tutsi can be regarded as distinct ethnic groups and how they developed in the course of history, and the answers both groups have found for it are important, as these answers have influenced the conflict so profoundly. They continue to play a role in Rwanda today and thus need to be examined carefully as a basis for any assessment of the reconciliation potential in Rwanda at present.[32] Furthermore it extracts the different myths circulating in Rwanda and the selective memories of each group. How do they influence perceptions of ethnicity, history and politics? To what extent are they relevant for reconciliation? Can there be reconciliation without a shared account of the past? Apart from the interpretation of past violence by different actors, chapter 3 will also present the current cleavages in Rwandan society and the ideology of national unity and "Rwandanness" by the RPF. Crucial questions in the context of RPF policies are: Is ethnicity the single defining characteristic in Rwandan society today? Does the banning of ethnicity by the RPF work or do people still identify strongly as Hutu and Tutsi? Is the idea of national unity encouraging reconciliation or rather prohibiting it?

In chapter 4 the political context of reconciliation is discussed. It will be analyzed in what way the authoritarian RPF government influences reconciliation. Can a minority regime effectively dictate reconciliation? To what extent does the image of the government to consist of mainly Tutsi play a role? The interpretation of history described in chapter 3 also plays a major role here. What impact does the imposition of a government reading of history have on the population? Can a top-down approach on reconciliation work? Furthermore it needs to be asked in what way the increasingly repressive style of government and the muzzling of opposition and press as well as intimidation of the population and disappearances influence the reconciliation process. Can reconciliation be achieved in a political climate characterized by repression? To answer these questions the reconciliation policies of the RPF and the self perception of the government are examined. Furthermore, the relevant political devel-

32 See Helmut Strizek: Kongo, Zaire – Ruanda – Burundi. Stabilität durch erneute Militärherrschaft? Studie zur „neuen Ordnung“ in Zentralafrika, München 1998, p. 55; Mahmood Mamdani: From Conquest to Consent as the Basis of State Formation. Reflections on Rwanda, in: New Left Review, Vol. 216 (1996) 1, p. 8.

opments and events from 1994 onwards are presented and special emphasis is laid on the growing authoritarianism of the regime. The slide towards a minority dictatorship and its impact on reconciliation is presented in greater detail. Finally the attitudes of the population towards the regime and the effects of repression on Rwandan society are made clear. The question whether minority rule coupled with an ideology of national unity can overcome the ethnic conflict will be answered at the end of the chapter.

Chapter 5 makes up the main body of this thesis. It outlines different approaches of transitional justice and explains the importance of justice for the reconciliation process in Rwanda. Ending the culture of impunity and actively acknowledging the past to prevent recourse to violence are important aspects here. It will then analyze the contribution of the ICTR, the national courts and the traditional Gacaca jurisdictions to reconciliation. The difference between retributive and restorative justice in transitional justice theory are presented as a basis for the analysis of justice in Rwanda. Restorative and retributive approaches to justice carry distinct features and present different strategies of dealing with the past through justice. The shift in government strategy from a purely vengeful approach in the beginning to a more restorative understanding of justice in recent years is made clear. First, the achievements of retributive justice for Rwanda's reconciliation are outlined before turning to the Gacaca jurisdictions as the new hope for justice and reconciliation. It will then also be discussed if a clear cut between retributive and restorative approaches in Rwanda is possible or if the Gacaca jurisdictions still bear some of the initial vengeful considerations.

The different forms of justice are analyzed with the following questions in mind: Have they been able to fulfil the Rwandan need for justice? Have they managed to establish truth about the events in 1994? Have they fostered acknowledgement, forgiveness and mutual understanding? Most importantly, have they restored ruptured relationships within Rwandan communities? The achievements and downfalls of all three approaches will be critically examined and evaluated to assess the reconciliatory potential of judicial approaches in Rwanda. Special emphasis is laid on Gacaca: Is Gacaca really "African Justice for African Healing"[33]? Can it achieve reconciliation more effectively than conventional justice? Is it really traditional, restorative and local? What implications do the answers on these questions have for their success? As it is too early to measure the success of judicial dealing with the past in Rwanda 14 years after the genocide this study will concentrate on the results that have been achieved so far and try to arrive at an assessment of their future potential.

---

33 Colin Waugh: Paul Kagame and Rwanda. Power, Genocide and the Rwandan Patriotic Front, Jefferson 2004, p. 173.

1.4 Literature Review

The body of literature on Rwanda in general is large and growing especially since the genocide and the following refugee crisis. Most scholars concentrate on the history of the country and the events in 1994 and the years afterwards. Usually emphasis is laid on explaining the genocide, the ethnic conflict, the role of the international community and the political situation, however, while the topic of reconciliation is not that well researched. It is mostly treated as a by-product of political and judicial processes and serves rarely as the main focus point. This paper aims at bringing existing literature from various fields such as law, political science, history, sociology and psychology together to explain the reconciliation process in Rwanda.

To outline the theoretical framework standard publications on the topic are used, mainly Martha Minow's "Between Vengeance and Forgiveness"[34] and John Paul Lederach's "Building Peace"[35], publications by the "Swedish International Development Agency" (SIDA)[36], the "International Institute for Democracy and Electoral Assistance" (IDEA)[37], the "Berghof Research Centre for Constructive Conflict Management"[38] as well as article collections by Nigel Biggar[39] and Martha Minow[40]. Harvard law professor Martha Minow analyzes responses to collective violence in several countries. Her book is a landmark in the field of dealing with the past, justice and healing. John Paul Lederach is one of the most famous experts in the field of conflict studies and the above mentioned book provides important insights in long term measures to achieve peace. The SIDA and IDEA reports offer a detailed analysis of different aspects of reconciliation and are essential to extract the main ingredients of a successful reconciliation processes. Several other articles complement the standard volumes, most importantly Ervin Staub's and Laurie Anne

---

34 Martha Minow: Between Vengeance and Forgiveness. Facing History after Genocide and Mass Violence, Boston 1998.

35 John Paul Lederach: Building Peace. Sustainable Reconciliation in Divided Societies, 7th edition, Washington D.C. 2006.

36 Karen Brounéus: Reconciliation. Theory and Practice for Development Cooperation, Stockholm 2003 (SIDA).

37 David Bloomfield/Teresa Barnes/Luc Huyse (eds.): Reconciliation After Violent Conflict. A Handbook, Stockholm 2003 (IDEA), in: http://www.idea.int/publications/reconciliation/upload/reconciliation_full.pdf (12.01.2008).

38 David Bloomfield/Martina Fischer/Beatrix Schmelzle(eds.): Berghof Handbook for Conflict Transformation, Berlin 2004, in: http://www.berghof-handbook.net/std_page.php?LANG=e&id=11 (02.06.2008).

39 Nigel Biggar (ed.): Burying the Past. Making Peace and Doing Justice After Violent Conflict, Washington D.C. 2003.

40 Antonia Chayes/Martha Minow (eds.): Imagine Coexistence. Restoring Humanity after Violent Ethnic Conflict, San Francisco et al. 2003.

Pearlman's research surveys in Rwanda that shed light on the psychological side of mass violence.[41]

On the history of the ethnic conflict and the politicization of ethnicity numerous books have been published. This thesis uses some of the standard volumes to explain the genesis of the ethnic conflict while neglecting some of the most known books on Rwandan history, as explaining the history is not the main focus of the analysis and the political implications of ethnicity are more important for the reconciliation process than purely historic accounts of the conflict. The works of Gérard Prunier[42] and Mahmood Mamdani[43] serve as the cornerstones of the description of ethnicity in Rwanda. While Prunier presents one of the best accounts of the Rwandan crisis and its historical roots, Ugandan political scientist Mahmood Mamdani gives an excellent insight in the relationship between ethnicity and politics in Rwanda in the past and today from an African perspective. Two other well known sources in German research circles are the article collection by Leonard Harding[44] and the works of Helmut Strizek[45]. The latter has to be judged carefully as he is very critical of the RPF and often differs in his analysis from other authors. Nevertheless his accounts of Rwandan history are a valuable source outside the main frame. Absolutely essential for highlighting the conflict background are Alison Des Forges' extensive work on the Rwandan genocide "Leave None to Tell the Story"[46] and the essay "Genocide in the Great Lakes" by renowned Rwanda specialist René Lemarchand[47]. Des Forges describes the Rwandan crisis in great detail and with a lot of information retrieved on the ground in Rwanda. Lemarchand's article is the best source of information on the different historical myths and selective memories in Rwanda. Apart from Mamdani this thesis

41 For example Ervin Staub/Laurie Anne Pearlman: Advancing Healing and Reconciliation, in: Laura Barbanel/Robert Sternberg (eds.): Psychological Interventions in Times of Crisis, New York 2006, pp. 213-243.

42 Gérard Prunier: The Rwanda Crisis 1959-1994. History of a Genocide, London 1995.

43 Mahmood Mamdani: When Victims Become Killers. Colonialism, Nativism, and the Genocide in Rwanda, 3rd edition, Princeton 2002.

44 Leonard Harding (ed.): Ruanda – der Weg zum Völkermord. Vorgeschichte, Verlauf, Deutung, Hamburg 1998.

45 For example Helmut Strizek: Ruanda und Burundi von der Unabhängigkeit zum Staatszerfall. Studien über eine gescheiterte Demokratie im afrikanischen Zwischenseengebiet, München 1996.

46 Alison Des Forges: Leave None to Tell the Story. Genocide in Rwanda, New York/Paris 1999.

47 René Lemarchand: Genocide in the Great Lakes. Which Genocide? Whose Genocide?, in: African Studies Review, Vol. 41 (1998) 1, pp. 3-16.

draws mainly on German Africa expert Rolf Hofmeier's[48] account of Rwandan society today to explain existing ethnic cleavages.
To describe the political system in Rwanda and the growing authoritarianism by the RPF the already mentioned volumes on reconciliation and history are used as well as works of Colin Waugh[49], Filip Reyntjens[50] and Alexander Stroh[51]. Reyntjens in particular is a well known expert on Rwanda and probably the scholar that has written most extensively and critically about political developments in Rwanda during the past years. Colin Waugh has analyzed the history of the RPF and its politics. His book is important to understand the RPF ideology and the reasons for its behaviour. In addition to these main sources and a number of other magazine articles, reports by independent "Non Governmental Organizations" (NGOs) like the "International Crisis Group"[52], "Human Rights Watch"[53] and "Amnesty International"[54] are used to highlight the current state of human rights and politics in Rwanda, as they deliver the most detailed picture of recent developments.
Literature on the main focus point of the thesis – the judicial approaches and their contribution to reconciliation – is abundant and continues to grow with the establishment of the Gacaca jurisdictions. However, the emphasis lies mostly on the international tribunal while the national court system is neglected. The Gacaca experiment has attracted the interest of scholars a lot recently but in the opinion of the author most recent contributions in that field have rather repeated previous findings than presented new aspects of the topic. Therefore the literature on this topic is narrowed down to the most interesting and important articles. Books on Gacaca are hard to find as the establishment of the Gacaca courts is a rather recent development.

---

48 Rolf Hofmeier: Soziokulturelle Kurzanalyse Ruanda, Hamburg 2005.

49 Colin Waugh: Paul Kagame and Rwanda. Power, Genocide and the Rwandan Patriotic Front, Jefferson 2004.

50 For example Filip Reynjens: Rwanda, Ten Years On. From Genocide to Dictatorship, in: African Affairs, Vol. 103 (2004) 411, pp. 177-210.

51 Stroh, Alexander: Legitimation allein durch Entwicklung? Das Beispiel Ruanda, Hamburg 2007 (GIGA Focus Afrika Nr. 11).

52 International Crisis Group: Rwanda at the End of the Transition. A Necessary Political Liberalisation, Nairobi/Brüssel 2002 (International Crisis Group Africa Report No 53), in: http://www.crisisgroup.org/library/documents/report_archive/A400817_13112002.pdf (02.01.2008).

53 For example Human Rights Watch: World Report 2008, New York et al. 2008, in: http://hrw.org/wr2k8/pdfs/wr2k8_web.pdf (16.05.2008).

54 Amnesty International: World Report 2007, London 2007, in: http://thereport.amnesty.org/document/15 (13.03.2008).

Uvin and Mironko[55], Alexander Betts[56], Paul Gready[57] and Lyn Graybill[58] deal with the different approaches to justice in Rwanda and analyze the differences, potentials and weaknesses of international, national and local forms of justice in the context of transitional justice. Helena Cobban[59] gives a practical insight in the work of the ICTR while Jackson Maogoto[60] sharply points out the weaknesses of the international court and its contribution to reconciliation. As extensive research on the national court system is lacking the above cited articles that deal with all forms of justice in Rwanda will be a main source. Stef Vandeginste's[61] contribution to Biggar's article collection also serves as an important background. Vandeginste has worked as a lawyer and for the UN in Rwanda and therefore provides an insider's look on justice in Rwanda.

Filip Reyntjens'[62] description of the traditional Gacaca courts before the genocide is the only research on that topic and therefore the main source used to explain the traditional model. "Penal Reform International" (PRI)[63] has accompanied the Gacaca experiment from the outset and several reports provide the most extensive analysis of advantages and shortcomings of the courts as well as information about changes and developments in the context of

55 Peter Uvin/Charles Mironko: Western and Local Approaches to Justice in Rwanda, in: Global Governance, Vol. 9 (2003), pp. 219-231.

56 Alexander Betts: Should Approaches to Post-Conflict Justice and Reconciliation Be Determined Globally, Nationally or Locally?, in: The European Journal of Development Research, Vol. 17 (2005) 4, pp. 735-752.

57 Paul Gready: Reconceptualising Transitional Justice. Embedded and Distanced Justice, in: Conflict, Security and Development, Vol. 5 (2005) 1, pp. 3-21.

58 Lyn S. Graybill: Pardon, Punishment, and Amnesia. Three African Post-conflict Methods, in: Third World Quarterly, Vol. 25 (2004) 6, pp. 1117-1130.

59 Helena Cobban: Healing Rwanda. Can an International Court Deliver Justice?, in: The Boston Review, Vol. 28 (2003) 5, in : http://bostonreview.net/BR28.6/cobban.html (16.02.2008).

60 Jackson Nyamuya Maogoto: The International Criminal Tribunal for Rwanda. A Distorting Mirror. Casting Doubt on its Actor Oriented Approach in Addressing the Rwandan Genocide, in: African Journal on Conflict Resolution, Vol. 3 (2003) 1, pp. 55-97, in: http://www.accord.org.za/ajcr/2003-1/accordr_v3_n1_a8.pdf (16.12.2007).

61 Stef Vandeginste: Rwanda. Dealing with Genocide and Crimes against Humanity in the Context of Armed Conflict and Failed Political Transition, in: Nigel Biggar (ed.): Burying the Past. Making Peace and Doing Justice After Violent Conflict, Washington D.C. 2003, pp. 251-285.

62 Filip Reyntjens: Le Gacaca ou la Justice du Gazon au Rwanda, in: Politique Africaine, Vol. 40 (1990), pp. 31-41, in: http://www.politique-africaine.com/numeros/pdf/040031.pdf (11.02.2008).

63 For example Penal Reform International: Integrated Report on Gacaca Research and Monitoring. Pilot Phase January 2002 – December 2004, London/Kigali 2005.

Gacaca. A study conducted by the John Hopkins University[64] highlights the perceptions of Rwandans regarding Gacaca and therefore helps to rate the acceptance of Gacaca in the Rwandan population. Erin Daly[65] critically examines Gacaca and reaches the conclusion that partial amnesty would be a better option. Allison Corey and Sandra Joireman[66] are also very sceptical of the ability of Gacaca to contribute to reconciliation. Jeremy Sarkin[67] calls for a truth and reconciliation commission as the appropriate answer for Rwanda, arguing from a South African perspective. Alana Tiemessen[68] on the other hand finds that despite the existing problems Gacaca has the potential to reconcile Rwandans. Uvin and Mironko also follow this view. Aneta Wierzynska[69] stresses the potential of Gacaca to strengthen democracy in Rwanda. It is along this spectre that the Gacaca jurisdictions are judged in the relatively small circle of international scholars dealing with the topic. The most extensive book published so far is Sandrine Schillings' "Gegen das Vergessen"[70] which analyzes Gacaca in terms of restorative and retributive justice. An important base for this area is also provided by American law scholar Marc Drumbl[71] who has written an excellent piece of work about shaming in dualist post-genocidal societies and abandoning ethnicity in favour of citizenship in Rwanda.

64 Simon Gabisirege/Stella Babalola: Perceptions About the Gacaca Law in Rwanda. Evidence From a Multi-Method Study, Baltimore 2001 (Special Publication No. 19 John Hopkins University School of Public Health), in : http://www.jhuccp.org/pubs/sp/19/English/19.pdf (12.06.3008).

65 Erin Daly: Between Punitive and Reconstructive Justice. The Gacaca Courts in Rwanda, in: Journal of International Law and Politics, Vol. 34 (2002) 2, pp. 355-396.

66 Allison Corey/Sandra Joireman: Retributive Justice. The Gacaca Courts in Rwanda, in: African Affairs, Vol. 103 (2004) 1, pp. 73-89.

67 Jeremy Sarkin: The Necessity and Challenges of Establishing a Truth and Reconciliation Commission in Rwanda, in: Human Rights Quarterly, Vol. 21 (1999) 3, pp. 776-823.

68 Alana Erin Tiemessen: After Arusha. Gacaca Justice in Post-Genocide Rwanda, in: African Studies Quarterly, Vol. 8 (2004) 1, pp. 57-76.

69 Aneta Wierzynska: Consolidating Democracy Through Rwanda's Transitional Gacaca Courts, in: New York University Law Review, Vol. 79 (2004) 5, pp. 1934-1969, in: http://www.law.nyu.edu/JOURNALS/LAWREVIEW/issues/vol79/no5/NYU508.pdf (15.03.2008).

70 Sandrine Schilling: Gegen das Vergessen. Justiz, Wahrheitsfindung und Versöhnung nach dem Genozid in Ruanda durch Mechanismen traditioneller Justiz. Gacaca Gerichte, Frankfurt am Main 2005.

71 Mark Antonin Drumbl: Punishment, Postgenocide. From Guilt to Shame to Civis in Rwanda, in: New York University Law Review, Vol. 75 (2000) 5, pp. 1221-1326.

It is important to keep in mind that the origins of the authors writing on Rwanda have a profound impact on their judgement of politics and justice in Rwanda. The cited contributions of Western scholars are certainly influenced by a Western understanding of political and legal processes. Western scholars will always examine a topic through their interpretative lens, which is framed by certain values and ideas developed by their own culture. This thesis tries to incorporate as many publications of African researchers as possible to establish a mixed picture of reconciliation in Rwanda, and the African justice mechanisms.

2 A theoretical framework of reconciliation

2.1 Reconciliation and coexistence

Internal conflicts like the one in Rwanda are characterized by deep-rooted fears and animosities between the conflicting groups that kept alive a cycle of violence over generations. The conflict parties usually live side by side and have profound negative stereotypes of their adversaries, coupled with direct traumatic experiences of violence.[72] These experiences and the extreme polarization of the groups have to be addressed if the country is not to fall into endless spirals of violence and become locked in a so called *conflict trap*.[73] There are various sources of hatred that keep these conflicts burning: oppression by the state, indoctrination by political and religious leaders, collective myths, economic dominance by one ethnic group over the other, social exclusion and previously committed violence that is still remembered by the victims.[74] All these factors hold true for the conflict in Rwanda. Trauma and intensive violence have been experienced by the majority of the Rwandese people and left deep scars on society. Due to the scale of violence and its profound impact in Rwanda the challenge of reconciliation is enormous.[75]

72 See Lederach: Building Peace, p. 23.

73 See Brounéus: Reconciliation. Theory and Practice for Development Cooperation, p. 9. The term *conflict trap* was developed to describe the phenomena that countries which have experienced civil war once are at risk to be subjected to war for years to come. Ending violence is difficult and even if peace is achieved it often remains fragile. These countries are trapped in cycles of violence that are likely to resurface after short periods of peace as fighting has become an end in itself. See: Paul Collier/V.L. Elliott/Harvard Hegre/Anke Hoeffler/Marta Reynal-Querol/Nicholas Sambanis: Breaking the Conflict Trap. Civil War and Development Policy, Washington D.C. 2003 (World Bank Policy Research Reports), pp. 79f.

74 See Sven M. Spengemann: Freedom's Hidden Price. Framing the Obstacles to Economic Coexistence, in: Antonia Chayes/Martha Minow (eds.): Imagine Coexistence. Restoring Humanity after Violent Ethnic Conflict, San Francisco et al. 2003, p. 147.

75 See David Bloomfield: The Context of Reconciliation, in: David Bloomfield/Teresa Barnes/Luc Huyse (eds.): Reconciliation After Violent Conflict. A Handbook, Stockholm 2003 (IDEA), in: http://www.idea.int/publications/reconciliation/upload/reconciliation_full.pdf (12.01.2008), p. 41.

2.1.1 Important aspects of reconciliation

Reconciliation is an aspect of transition to democracy and conflict resolution theory that has gained broader attention by scholars only fairly recently. There exist, however, no agreements on how the term reconciliation is to be defined.[76] Many definitions include restoration of relationships in their understanding of reconciliation. Social relationships need to be repaired and negative relationships overcome with the desired outcome being the re-establishment of former friendship and peace and at least a minimal degree of trust.[77] This can only happen when members of both groups, victimized and perpetrator, consider themselves to belong to the same group or category. This category must supersede the in-group each person identifies with; people need to, for example, regard each other as human beings rather than members of ethnic groups.[78] Human dignity as well as basic human rights and respect are fundamental values that serve as a basis for the restoration of relationships between people in order to achieve reconciliation.[79] A typical African notion of humanness is *ubuntu*, a concept associated with South Africa but widely shared on the African continent. *Ubuntu* means "a person is a person through other people"[80]. The individual therefore is obliged to share and participate, as no human being stands alone but is part of a community. The community's right to peace is viewed as higher than the individual's right to punish others for their wrongdoing. Understanding and reparation are therefore more important than revenge and retaliation, as the former can contribute to mending relationships that have been destroyed.[81] Accordingly, reconciliation in the

---

76 See Zorbas: Reconciliation in Post-genocide Rwanda, p. 30.

77 See Lederach: Building Peace, p. 26; Jörg Lehmann: Thesenpapier zur Trauma-Arbeit im Kontext des Zivilen Friedensdienstes, insbesondere bei Versöhnungsprozessen, Bonn 2007 (Thesenpapier des Referats P10 im DED), p. 2; David Bloomfield: Reconciliation. An Introduction, p. 11.

78 See Michael J.A. Wohl/Nyla R. Branscombe: Forgiving the Ingroup or the Outgroup for Harm Doing, in: American Psychological Association (ed.): Forgiveness. A Sampling of Research Results (Compiled by the American Psychological Association on the Occasion of the 59th Annual DPI/NGO Conference United Nations Headquarters, Midday Workshop "*Forgiveness: Partnering with the Enemy*"), Washington 2006, in: http://www.apa.org/international/un-forgive.pdf (12.01.2008), p. 20.

79 See Natascha Zupan/Sylvia Servaes: Transitional Justice and Dealing with the Past, Bonn 2007 (Frient Guidance Paper Transitional Justice), in: http://www.frient.de/downloads/FriEnt_Guidance%20Paper%20Transitional%20Justice_2007.pdf (12.01.2008), p. 4.

80 Desmond Tutu: No Future Without Forgiveness, London et al. 1999, p. 35.

81 See Graybill: Pardon, Punishment, and Amnesia, pp. 1118f.

Rwandan language Kinyarwanda, *ubwiyunge*, means "bringing people together whose relationships have been ruptured"[82].

Another important aspect of reconciliation is time. Most sources agree that reconciliation is a long-term process that involves long-term measures to succeed and will take generations to complete.[83] Paul Lederach defines reconciliation as a focus and a locus at the same time. It is a place where adversaries can meet and acknowledge the past in order to envision a future and reassess the present. And it is also the goal to achieve in the long term perspective, the shared focus of people envisioning reconciliation.[84] It is therefore in David Bloomfield's words "a process through which a society moves from a divided past to a shared future"[85]. This process entails, according to Carlos Sluzki, six successive steps that comprise conflict, coexistence, collaboration, cooperation, interdependence and finally integration. Each step is characterized by certain attitudes towards the other group. While hostility dominates in the beginning, it is followed by resentment and mistrust at the next step that gives way for ambivalence on the third level. Cooperation then develops careful empathy and interdependence cautious trust, which is transformed into friendly trust at the integration level.[86]

Official acknowledgement of the suffering inflicted on victims is vital to prepare the grounds for reconciliation.[87] Often this requires a change in attitudes

---

82 Annemiek Richters/Cora Dekker/Klaas de Jonge: Reconciliation in the Aftermath of Violent Conflict in Rwanda, in: Intervention, Vol. 3 (2005) 3, p. 218.

83 See Luc Huyse: The Process of Reconciliation, in: David Bloomfield/Teresa Barnes/Luc Huyse (eds.): Reconciliation After Violent Conflict. A Handbook, Stockholm 2003 (IDEA), in: http://www.idea.int/publications/reconciliation/upload/reconciliation_full.pdf (12.01.2008), p. 28; Brounéus: Reconciliation. Theory and Practice for Development Cooperation, p. 49; Lehmann: Thesenpapier, p. 9.

84 See Lederach: Building Peace, pp. 27ff.

85 Bloomfield: Reconciliation. An Introduction, p. 12.

86 See Carlos E. Sluzki: The Process Toward Reconciliation, in: Antonia Chayes/Martha Minow (eds.): Imagine Coexistence. Restoring Humanity after Violent Ethnic Conflict, San Francisco et al. 2003, p. 23.
Hizkias Assefa also establishes reconciliation as the last step in the spectrum of mechanisms to deal with violent conflict. In his model force, adjudication, arbitration, negotiation, mediation and reconciliation are successive steps along a line of reactive and proactive measures in the search for a solution of the conflict; See: Hizkias Assefa: The Meaning of Reconciliation, in: European Centre for Conflict Prevention, in: http://www.gppac.net/documents/pbp/part1/2_reconc.htm (13.03.2008), [Subsection 1].

87 See Gunnar Theissen: Supporting Justice, Coexistence and Reconciliation After Armed Conflict. Strategies for Dealing with the Past, in: David Bloomfield/Martina Fischer/Beatrix Schmelzle (eds.): Berghof Handbook for Conflict Transformation, Berlin 2004, in: http://www.berghof-handbook.net/uploads/download/theissen_handbook.pdf (16.12.2007), p. 2.

towards the other group, especially when a military defeat put an end to violence.[88] Transforming beliefs and improving attitudes and emotions are of crucial importance in conflicts where mutual violence is so intractable that they cannot be resolved peacefully otherwise. Relationships will continue to be haunted by the past if this transformation fails.[89] It would be naïve to expect reconciliation to come naturally and promptly, however, as the development of a new social thinking takes time and must be accompanied by various interdependent factors like justice, healing and forgiveness.[90]
Finally, there is a difference to be made between the individual and collective level of these processes. While certain measures and steps can be taken in the political sphere to enhance reconciliation, this kind must be deemed national or political reconciliation. Reconciliation processes on the individual level are complex and deeply personal and it is questionable whether they can be influenced by political means.[91] On the other hand it is assumed that individual reconciliation in South Africa has led to reconciliation on the national level.[92] Huyse argues that interpersonal reconciliation as the development of trust between victim and perpetrator necessarily demands reconciliation of different groups and within communities, as the personal restoration will not work without taking the social environment into account and seeking to repair relationships on a broader level.[93]
In a rather minimalist notion of the concept the mentioned book by Martha Minow and Antonia Chayes concentrates on coexistence rather than reconciliation. They deem it easier to achieve in the aftermath of mass violence, when asking forgiveness or reconciliation seems to insult the victims still deeply wounded by the loss of their loved ones. Coexistence in this sense requires not only peaceful cohabitation but at least some kind of cooperation between adversary ethnic groups.[94] The term "coexistence", however, is used

88 See Alexander Gubin/Athanase Hagengimana/Laurie Anne Pearlman/Ervin Staub: Healing, Reconciliation, Forgiving and the Prevention of Violence After Genocide or Mass Killing. An Intervention and its Experimental Evaluation in Rwanda, in: Journal of Social and Clinical Psychology, Vol. 24 (2005) 3, p. 300.

89 See Bronéus: Reconciliation. Theory and Practice for Development Cooperation, p. 15.

90 See Reinhardt: Signs of Hope after the Genocide, p. 196.

91 See Bronéus: Reconciliation. Theory and Practice for Development Cooperation, p. 14; Laurel E. Fletcher/Harvey M. Weinstein: Violence and Social Repair. Rethinking the Contribution of Justice to Reconciliation, in: Human Rights Quarterly, Vol. 24 (2002) 3, p. 637.

92 See Graybill: Pardon, Punishment and Amnesia, p. 1120.

93 See Huyse: The Process of Reconciliation, p. 22.

94 See Antonia Chayes/Martha Minow: Introduction, in: Antonia Chayes/Martha Minow (eds.): Imagine Coexistence. Restoring Humanity after Violent Ethnic Conflict, San Francisco et al. 2003, p. xx.

as widely and variably as the term "reconciliation". While it can simply mean "living side by side without returning to violent conflict resolution such as killing the other", it might also describe a completely integrated society as in the last step of Sluzki's model towards reconciliation.[95] It therefore does not serve as a more stringent basis for the assessment of transitional developments in Rwanda than reconciliation. Even though it might be a more feasible goal than reconciliation[96] the importance of the term reconciliation in the Rwandan context makes it a more appropriate definition to use.

In an attempt to bring together different definitions of reconciliation this chapter concludes with the most essential points that surround the concept of reconciliation. Timothy Longman et al. define "community", "interdependence", "social justice" and "non-violence" as basic pillars of reconciliation. Groups as well as individuals and the state must envision a shared future, learn to work together across former divisions, embrace human rights and democratic values and solve conflicts without recourse to violence.[97] Karen Bronéus emphasizes three dimensions, drawing on van der Merwe, namely relationships, substantive elements like truth and justice and social elements that lead to the restoration of a positive and sustainable peace.[98] Hizkias Assefa defines acknowledgement of injuries and remorse, apologies for the personal role played in the conflict, overcoming bitter feelings developed through the conflict, the commitment not to return to violent means used during the conflict, compensation of victims, healing past grievances and the development of new relationships as core elements of reconciliation.[99]

Reconciliation as a political concept does not mean that conflicting parties must share the same beliefs and pursue the same interests, however. It rather requires people to let go of the assumption that their fellow citizens are enemies and therefore conflicts can only be resolved by violent means. Adversaries need to learn that they share a common political space. Certain political

---

95 See Aneelah Afzali/Laura Colleton: Constructing Coexistence. A Survey of Coexistence Projects in Areas of Ethnic Conflict, in: Antonia Chayes/Martha Minow (eds.): Imagine Coexistence. Restoring Humanity after Violent Ethnic Conflict, San Francisco et al. 2003, p. 3.

96 See Elizabeth V. Spelman: Coexistence and Repair, in: Antonia Chayes/Martha Minow (eds.): Imagine Coexistence. Restoring Humanity after Violent Ethnic Conflict, San Francisco et al. 2003, p. 243.

97 See Timothy Longman/Phuong Pham/Harvey Weinstein: Connecting Justice to Human Experience. Attitudes Towards Accountability and Reconciliation in Rwanda, in: Eric Stover et al. (eds.): My Neighbour, My Enemy. Justice and Community in the Aftermath of Mass Atrocity, Cambridge 2004, p. 207.

98 See Bronéus, Reconciliation. Theory and Practice for Development Cooperation, p. 16.

99 See Assefa: The Meaning of Reconciliation, [Subsection: What does Reconciliation entail].

and ethical values frame that shared space of which everyone is a part.[100] It is important to note that the meaning of reconciliation, when applied in a political context like the Rwanda crisis this thesis deals with, is altered and shifted from an individual to a collective process and entails peaceful coexistence and an end to fighting.[101] Real reconciliation in a political sense will lead to political stability. In that respect mending interpersonal relationships is not sufficient. Overcoming hardened group identities and dealing with past injuries needs the development of not only social and personal ties, but also new political relationships. It must not be forgotten that perpetrators and victims have different perceptions of reconciliation; and strategies to deal with the past will not gain the same support of all groups involved.[102] As mentioned before, truth and justice are such strategies of dealing with the past and pursuing reconciliation. However, neither can achieve reconciliation on its own.[103] Both are key ingredients of the process and will therefore be discussed in detail in subsequent chapters.

At this point it is necessary to include the Christian notion of reconciliation, as Rwanda is a very religious country and religion automatically influences political attempts to reconcile the population. The Christian definition of the term holds that reconciliation comes from God. All strategies developed towards reconciliation are therefore only carried out as God's agents. As God first turns to the victim, strategies that focus on the perpetrators and stress the acknowledgement of wrongs are considered false. Reconciliation in a Christian sense cannot start with the evil doer, but with the victim.[104]

2.1.2 Healing and the process of reconciliation

It has been argued that healing and reconciliation are interrelated processes. Healing of inflicted wounds will prevent recourse to violence and prepare the grounds for reconciliation and a changed psychological orientation towards the other which is a prerequisite for reconciliation. The process of healing is

---

100 See Jean Bethke Elshtain: Politics and Forgiveness, in: Nigel Biggar (ed.): Burying the Past. Making Peace and Doing Justice After Violent Conflict, Washington D.C. 2003, p. 59.

101 See Pankhurst: Issues of Justice and Reconciliation in Complex Political Emergencies, pp. 240ff.

102 See Judy Barsalou: Trauma and Transitional Justice in Divided Societies, Washington D.C. 2005 (USIP Special Report Nr. 135), p. 10.

103 See Bloomfield: Reconciliation. An Introduction, p. 14.

104 See Brian Starken (ed.): Working for Reconciliation. A Caritas Handbook, Vatikan City 1999, in: http://www.caritas.org/static/pdf/eng/wkgreconc.pdf (12.01.2008), p. 31.

not restricted to victims, however, perpetrators are in need of healing too.[105] As they tend to justify their violent behavior in order to avoid facing their own horrible deeds, healing can help perpetrators to stop blaming the victims and instead arrive at acknowledging their humanity. Humanizing victims through a process of healing enables them to regret and open themselves for reconciliation.[106] But traumatized victims in particular have to understand that the genocide is a past event and not a present reality anymore.[107]

The individual healing process and the healing of the nation at large is not the same.[108] But processes on the individual and collective level to overcome trauma influence each other. Individual trauma is one aspect of collective experiences of violence, which have destroyed any values and norms that used to regulate social relationships. Neither the individual nor the society seems capable of developing visions for the future as a consequence of trauma directly after the conflict. Inner healing leads to internalized peace and an internal reconciliation with past events, but acknowledgement and reparation by society are also crucial to achieve reconciliation in the long run.[109]

Brandon Hambers questions in this context the use of medical language like "*post-traumatic stress disorder*" (PTSD) in the healing process, as addressing these symptoms is in itself not helpful to address the roots of the violence.[110] Barsalou rejects the inclusion of terms like trauma and healing in the reconciliation process altogether and argues that more attention needs to be diverted to the reconstruction of society, as rule of law and security will create the necessary psychological conditions for individuals to regain control of their lives.[111] Indeed, if healing is the predominant term used in the discourse of mass violence, the emphasis lies on trauma and health rather than justice and dealing with the past, which will be the paradigms employed in this work.[112]

---

105 See Gubin/Hagengimana/Pearlman/Staub: Healing, Reconciliation, Forgiving and the Prevention of Violence after Genocide or Mass Killing, pp. 300ff.

106 See Staub/Pearlman: Advancing Healing and Reconciliation, p. 216.

107 See David Becker: Ohne Hass keine Versöhnung. Das Trauma der Verfolgten, Freiburg 1992, p. 231.

108 See Brandon Hamber: Does the Truth Heal? A Psychological Perspective on Political Strategies for Dealing With the Legacy of Political Violence, in: Nigel Biggar (ed.): Burying the Past. Making Peace and Doing Justice After Violent Conflict, Washington D.C. 2003, p. 162.

109 See Lehmann: Thesenpapier, pp. 1ff.

110 See Brandon Hamber: Healing, in: David Bloomfield/Teresa Barnes/Luc Huyse (eds.): Reconciliation After Violent Conflict. A Handbook, Stockholm 2003 (IDEA), in: http://www.idea.int/publications/reconciliation/upload/reconciliation_full.pdf (12.01.2008), p. 79.

111 See Barsalou: Trauma and Transitional Justice in Divided Societies, p. 5.

112 See Minow: Between Vengeance and Forgiveness, p. 63.

Whatever argument one follows, it is clear that inner healing and societal reconciliation processes can often be at odds. Political processes can certainly create the conditions for victims to heal, but individual healing does not necessarily unfold at the same pace as the national reconciliation process. This can result in victims opposing reconciliation, as it is perceived as false when traumatized persons are not yet ready to move on.[113]

2.2 Key issues of reconciliation

2.2.1 The relationship between forgiveness and reconciliation

Forgiveness can be defined as a change in attitude by a hurt person where he or she abstains from revenge and instead turns feelings of anger and hatred into a more positive orientation towards the perpetrator.[114] Two lines of argument can be followed in the discussion about forgiveness and reconciliation. They can either be viewed as separate processes in that forgiveness is not a prerequisite of reconciliation. Forgiveness then is a process involving only one person, being the victim, while reconciliation requires mutual changes in both parties. If the perpetrator is not included in this one-way process, forgiveness can happen independently of reconciliation, requiring only the victim to change his attitude towards the wrong-doer.[115] Or forgiveness can be, as in a Christian understanding of reconciliation, fundamental for reconciliation. Forgiveness then is a mutual process, requiring repentance by the perpetrator and forgiveness of the victim to achieve reconciliation.[116] There are indications that Rwandans might be inclined to enshrine this latter notion of forgiveness, as studies by Ervin Staub and others have shown that recipients expect acknowledgement and remorse in exchange for forgiveness.[117]
Forgiveness can be a value in itself. This view is often propagated by people involved in the "South African Truth and Reconciliation Commission" (TRC)

---

113 See Hambers: Healing, p. 80.

114 See Ervin Staub/Laurie Anne Pearlman: Promoting Reconciliation and Forgiveness after Mass Violence. Rwanda and Other Settings, in: American Psychological Association (ed.): Forgiveness. A Sampling of Research Results (Compiled by the American Psychological Association on the Occasion of the 59th Annual DPI/NGO Conference United Nations Headquarters, Midday Workshop "*Forgiveness: Partnering with the Enemy*"), Washington 2006, in: http://www.apa.org/international/un-forgive.pdf (12.01.2008), p. 24.

115 See Karen Brounéus: Reconciliation and Development, Berlin 2007 (FES Dialogue on Globalization. Occasional Papers Berlin Nr. 36), p. 6.

116 See Starken: Working for Reconciliation, p. 36.

117 See Gubin/Hagengimana/Pearlman/Staub: Healing, Reconciliation, Forgiving and the Prevention of Violence after Genocide or Mass Killing, p. 325.

established after apartheid. It can be a means to build bridges to other humans and let go of hatred and fury without forgetting what has happened.[118] It is therefore in people's best interest to forgive as it overcomes the dehumanization inflicted on the victim by the violence of the perpetrators and helps to survive the gruesome experiences of the past.[119] In this sense forgiveness contributes to healing. But forgiveness is also closely connected to its opposite twin: vengeance. As forgiveness is not a substitute for punishment, victims can still wish to prosecute the perpetrator after they have granted forgiveness. This is in fact a healthy process as forgiveness in concrete political circumstances often leads to amnesty, and, as a consequence, to amnesia. In that case the injury is not forgiven but ignored and will eventually return to haunt society. Therefore forgiveness must not be equated with forgetfulness.[120]

Societal forgiveness should not be confused with individual forgiveness. Society can opt for forgiving perpetrators to allow for reintegration of this group into the community but the individual victim cannot be forced to forgive. It might be too early for victims to take that step and pressures to do so might further crush the victim's self-esteem. Calls to stop hating each other in a top-down manner are therefore not desirable and likely to be fruitless. Forgiveness might emerge some time in the future but should not be an outspoken goal in direct post-conflict reconciliation efforts.[121]

2.2.2 The importance of truth

For the members of the TRC in South Africa, truth is the central ingredient of reconciliation. If reconciliation implies that a violent past is not repeated and cycles of revenge be ended, the truth about this past needs to be brought to light so that people have the safety they need to build a confidence in the future and leave that past behind.[122] As Donald W. Shriver, argues: "We can change our relation to the past, and the first step for doing so is uncovering its dreaded secrets. There can be no final burying of the past without an in-

---

118 See Pumla Gobodo-Madikizela: Trauma und Versöhnung. Lehren aus Südafrika, in: Aus Politik und Zeitgeschichte, (2006) 42, p. 36.

119 See Tutu: No Future Without Forgiveness, p. 35.

120 See Minow: Between Vengeance and Forgiveness, p. 15.

121 See Bronéus: Reconciliation. Theory and Practice for Development Cooperation, pp. 18f.

122 See Desmond Tutu: Foreword, in: David Bloomfield/Teresa Barnes/Luc Huyse (eds.): Reconciliation After Violent Conflict. A Handbook, Stockholm 2003 (IDEA), in: http://www.idea.int/publications/reconciliation/upload/reconciliation_full.pdf (12.01.2008), p. 4.

quest."[123] The assumption here is not only that testimonies by victims and perpetrators can heal the individual, but also the society as a whole.[124] Truth is needed to establish what has actually happened and often it is more important for survivors than justice. It is also needed to build a new society out of the ashes of an oppressive regime based on lies.[125]

There is no data confirming the positive influence of truth and its contribution to reconciliation. Nevertheless truth is commonly regarded as crucial by many experts as it makes denial of the facts impossible and can help to build the trust needed to reach the top of the ladder in a reconciliation process. On the other hand truth may open old wounds and bring back deeply buried painful memories. Thus revealing is not automatically healing, as the slogan of the TRC in South Africa claimed. There is a potential risk that reopening wounds may lead to re-traumatization or even renewed violence.[126] Despite this risk, the desire for truth among victims and their relatives is enormous. Knowing the truth may be painful, but it firstly helps relatives to face the facts, bury their hopes and achieve closure. Secondly it allows the victim to understand her suffering and come to terms with it.[127]

Acknowledgement of the past and the views on reconciliation and truth are of course likely to vary between conflicting groups, the perpetrator group being resentful towards calls for truth while the victim group may demand it.[128] Furthermore, there is not only one truth. It is usually distinguished between objective, subjective and intersubjective truth. While objective truth is regarded as factual, scholars have come to conclude that facts cannot bridge divides in societies as it is the interpretation of facts that matters. This is where intersubjective truth comes into play, especially in cases like Rwanda where interpretation patterns vary considerably between groups. Intersubjective truth, how-

---

123 Donald W. Shriver: Where and When in Political Life Is Justice Served by Forgiveness?, in: Nigel Biggar (ed.): Burying the Past. Making Peace and Doing Justice After Violent Conflict, Washington D.C. 2003, p. 28.

124 See Minow: Between Vengeance and Forgiveness, p. 61.

125 See Starken: Working for Reconciliation, p. 36.

126 See Bronéus: Reconciliation. Theory and Practice for Development Cooperation, pp. 27 and 37.

127 See Nigel Biggar: Making Peace or Doing Justice. Must We Choose?, in: Nigel Biggar (ed.): Burying the Past. Making Peace and Doing Justice After Violent Conflict, Washington D.C. 2003, p. 9. A prominent example of that desire is Apartheid victim Reverend Frank Chikane: "'The healing for me is the knowledge. It's not the prosecution, it's not the imprisonment. It's that you've come to me and said 'I'm sorry, I did it.'" Cited in David Goodman: Fault Lines. Journeys Into the New South Africa, Berkeley et al. 1999, p. 65.

128 See Staub/Pearlman: Advancing Healing and Reconciliation, p. 232.

ever, is only possible when different versions of the past are allowed and not only one dominant narrative shapes the discourse about the past.[129]
In political transitions choices have to be made regarding truth and its relation to justice. Without truth, Gerd Hankel claims, there will be no justice. And without justice, there will be no reconciliation.[130] But justice in moral terms is not necessarily justice established by a court, and therefore several questions need to be asked. Can legal courts establish truth and if so, what kind of truth? Is it more important to punish wrong or to arrive at knowledge?[131] South Africa has answered this question in opting for truth, the path of Rwanda remains to be seen.

2.2.3 The contribution of justice and dealing with the past to reconciliation

Literature about dealing with the past seems to unavoidably quote philosopher George Santayana's saying that "those who cannot remember the past are condemned to repeat it."[132] Desmond Tutu refers to that saying when he claims that the past will unavoidably come back to haunt us: "Unless we look the beast in the eye we will find that it returns to hold us hostage."[133]
As much as dealing with the past as a condition for peace, the need for justice is widely acknowledged as a condition for reconciliation. In a post-conflict situation three aspects of justice seem important: Rule of law and the restoration of the judicial system are necessary conditions for security and stability, addressing the conflict and the suffering it has inflicted is vital for peace and healing of victims, and investigating the root causes of the conflict such as economic injustice can prevent renewed conflict.[134]
Justice, however, is easily seen as vengeance, especially if large segments of the population have been involved in violence. It seems clear that a history of violence, coupled with impunity, cries out for a judicial answer. Yet the kind of answer has to be carefully examined. Examining the past inevitably opens new wounds, and sometimes this can prove risky for peace and reconciliation. On

---

129 See Tuomas Forsberg: The Philosophy and Practice of Dealing With the Past. Some Conceptual and Normative Issues, in: Nigel Biggar (ed.): Burying the Past. Making Peace and Doing Justice After Violent Conflict, Washington D.C. 2003, p. 73.

130 See Gerd Hankel: Vergangenheit, die nicht ruhen darf. Essay, in: Aus Politik und Zeitgeschichte, (2006) 42, p. 7.

131 See Minow: Between Vengeance and Forgiveness, p. 87.

132 George Santayana: Life of Reason or The Phases of Human Progress. By George Santayana 2, London 1905, p. 284.

133 Tutu: No Future Without Forgiveness, p. 31.

134 See Bronéus: Reconciliation. Theory and Practice for Development Cooperation, pp. 28f.

the other hand peace may only be restored when justice is being done, and more importantly seen to be done by a population used to see impunity fester. Whether or not reconciliation can develop out of this kind of justice, which often manifests itself in mass trials, is questionable. Mass prosecutions might be counterproductive. The fact that the kind of justice opted for is a political choice, and that decisions about who is prosecuted and what crimes are punished is highly political, make the endeavor all the more difficult.[135] Helena Cobban, too, regards reconciliation as an explicit political, and not judicial, matter. But as dealing with past injustices is such an important part of the reconciliation process, courts might be able to assist the complex process of reconciliation.[136]

Hizkias Assefa stresses that justice is an integral part of reconciliation, and a basic condition. But justice itself is not sufficient, and if it is justice in the common punitive sense, it will not contribute to creating a shared future for former enemies, and thus to reconciliation. Change in attitudes, different behavior and ending hatred is therefore best achieved by what has come to be known as restorative justice, which is not just occupied with punishing offenders, but restoration of society.[137] But, as Wolfgang Rheinhardt argues, punishing gruesome acts is necessary, even if the act has been forgiven. Punishment does not contradict reconciliation, or forgiveness. A victim can offer forgiveness and still demand justice.[138] This is basically the line that is being followed in Rwanda as will be shown in chapter five, where different approaches of transitional justice will be dealt with.

It seems important to note that reconciliation means very different things to different groups, and that touches the issue of justice, too. While perpetrators may view amnesty as a necessary condition for reconciliation, traumatized victims are preoccupied with vengeance and therefore punishment as an appropriate consequence of violence.[139] But, as Gunnar Theißen has argued, victims have to learn that justice can never be done in a comprehensive way. Practical constraints and political power structures and choices will influence justice. It might be a major obstacle to reconciliation if adequate justice is lacking for real world reasons.[140] Justice may not be sufficient, but nevertheless it is at the

135 See Pankhurst: Issues of Justice and Reconciliation in Complex Political Emergencies, p. 242.

136 See Helena Cobban: The Legacies of Collective Violence. The Rwandan Genocide and the Limits of Law, in: The Boston Review, Vol. 27 (2002) 2, in: http://bostonreview.net/BR27.2/cobban.html (16.02.2008), [Subsection 1].

137 See Assefa: The Meaning of Reconciliation, [Subsection Reconciliation and Justice].

138 See Reinhardt: Signs of Hope after the Genocide, p. 199.

139 See Forsberg: The Philosophy and Practice of Dealing With the Past, p. 73.

140 See Theissen: Supporting Justice, Coexistence and Reconciliation After Armed Conflict, p. 16.

core of reconciliation, especially as far as victims are concerned. It is probably also the most measurable contribution to reconciliation in the political sphere, while it also sheds lights on the inner-personal reconciliation processes. This is why the author has deemed it as an appropriate focus point of this thesis.

2.3 Reconciliation in theory: A conclusion

The theories and definitions about reconciliation presented serve as the basis for the analysis of the Rwandan situation. David Bloomfield's definition about the creation of a shared future from a divided past is highly applicable to Rwanda. After this violent past is analyzed and thus the luggage each Rwandan carries with him in the reconciliation process becomes clear, the developed framework will be used to examine reconciliation in Rwanda. It has been shown that justice is a key ingredient of any reconciliation process. Truth and acknowledgement of the past are important aspects here. Victims need the truth to heal, and acknowledgement on behalf of the perpetrators can empower them and allow them to move on with their life as a full member of society. Acknowledgement is also crucial to facilitate a change in attitudes in both parties. Furthermore, it is important to examine the past as a basis for future peace. Societies need to face their deeds to avoid repeating the violent past. *Vergangenheitsbewältigung* is crucial for a peaceful future.

This chapter has explained the importance of restored relationships, the commitment to non-violence and remorse as a basis for forgiveness and reconciliation. Forgiveness in Rwanda can be facilitated through signs of repentance by perpetrators but is an individual, long-term process that cannot be rushed by outsiders. The same holds true for healing, which can be facilitated through measures aiming at reconciliation, but is likely to remain a highly personal process. It can be at odds with political reconciliation processes. But reconciliation is nevertheless a political affair, as it also includes the commitment of former adversaries to share a common political space.

Reconciliation is a long term process. Thus it will be impossible to determine to what extent Rwanda has achieved reconciliation today. But assessing the potential of Gacaca jurisdictions and criminal courts to contribute to creating a shared future with reconciled accounts of the past, peaceful coexistence, acknowledgement and forgiveness, and to a small extent also healing, can show how far Rwanda has come on the path to reconciliation in a judicial and political sense.

3 The Rwanda crisis: Inventing ethnicity

3.1 The history of ethnitization in Rwanda

The Rwanda crisis as well as its spitting image Burundi is commonly regarded as an ethnic conflict between the bipolar groups of Hutu and Tutsi, with the third group Twa not playing a dominant role. The history of this conflict that culminated in the genocide in 1994, traces back much longer than the civil war at the beginning of the 1990s.[141] The roots and origins of Rwanda's problems today are a heavily contested issue. Different versions of the country's history are upheld by the different social groups as well as numerous scholars that specialize on Rwanda. Who bears how much guilt, which group is accused of greater evil and how history needs to be interpreted is an issue of heated debates. Every scholar dealing with Rwanda needs to be aware of the fact that his work will be judged by the perceived position he takes and that it is impossible to avoid being categorized.[142] It is not the aim of this thesis to give a detailed account of Rwanda's contested history.[143] The main facts will be dealt with briefly in the following chapters.

3.1.1 Hutu and Tutsi in pre-colonial times

Most scholars agree that Hutu, Tutsi and Twa existed as three distinct groups when the first Europeans arrived.[144] There are various theories about the different origins of these groups with the "Hamite theory" being the most famous. It claims that the Tutsi migrated to Rwanda from Ethiopia while the Hutu were the indigenous dwellers to Rwandan soil. While Wolfgang Rheinhardt suggests that this legend was known inside Rwanda before coloni-

---

141 See André Guichaoua: La région des Grands Lacs. Un lourd passé, un présent dramatique, un avenir des plus sombres, in: André Guichaoua (ed.): Les Crises Politiques au Burundi et au Rwanda (1993-1994). Analyses, Faits et Documents, 2nd edition, Paris 1995, p. 19.

142 See Prunier: The Rwanda Crisis, p. 157; Corey/Joireman: Retributive Justice, p. 74.

143 For detailed examinations of Rwanda's history see the works of Mamdani, Guichaoua, Chretien or Newbury: Catherine Newbury: The Cohesion of Oppression. Clientship and Ethnicity in Rwanda. 1860-1960, New York 1988; Jean-Pierre Chrétien: The Great Lakes of Africa. Two Thousand Years of History, New York 2003; André Guichaoua (ed.): Les Crises Politiques au Burundi et au Rwanda (1993-1994). Analyses, Faits et Documents, 2nd edition, Paris 1995; Mahmood Mamdani: When Victims Become Killers. Colonialism, Nativism, and the Genocide in Rwanda, 3rd edition, Princeton 2002.

144 See for example Prunier: The Rwanda Crisis, p. 5; Strizek: Ruanda und Burundi von der Unabhängigkeit zum Staatszerfall, p. 38.

zation, it developed its influence only later.[145] A report by PRI claims that the migration theory has to be scientifically dismissed, as an ethnic conscience of the different groups in Rwanda was built up progressively in the course of state formation.[146] But some scholars believe that migration nevertheless took place in Rwanda. Contrary to the "Hamite theory" they suggest that both groups, not only the Tutsi, migrated to the area centuries ago with the Twa being the only indigenous group.[147] Apart from migration, differences between the groups were also explained by the so-called "nutrition theory", which claimed that Tutsi got their distinct features from their rich diet while the Twa and Hutu stayed small due to their eating habits. It is impossible to tell what is fact or fiction in the light of the many stories that circulate about Rwanda.[148]

Whatever the case, even if the groups migrated at different times in the course of history, they became one cultural community that spoke the same language – Kinyarwanda – intermarried and lived together both inside and outside of Rwanda.[149] The country was ruled by an absolute monarchy and the origins of that dynasty can be traced back to the 15th century.[150] The aristocracy consisted of Tutsi with the Tutsi king being the highest authority and the Nyiginya and Bega clans the dominant aristocratic groups at the court.[151]

Cyprian Fisiy argues that Rwandese society was flexible. Hutu could become Tutsi and vice versa; intermarriage blurred the lines between the two groups even further. The only difference consisted in the occupation of the two groups. While Tutsi were pastoralists, Hutu usually were farming the land.[152] Mamdani dismisses the notion that a socio-economic distinction existed because one group of Tutsi, known as *petits Tutsi*, had no cattle as well, and thus he deems as a myth that the distinction between the groups was one of rich

---

145 See Reinhardt: Signs of Hope After the Genocide, p. 189; Katrin Wissbar: Guter Hutu - Böser Tutsi. Der Aufstieg der Hutu Power, in: Leonard Harding (ed.): Ruanda – der Weg zum Völkermord. Vorgeschichte, Verlauf, Deutung, Hamburg 1998, p. 127.

146 See Penal Reform International: Research Report on the Gacaca. Report VI. From Camp to Hill, the Reintegration of Released Prisoners, Paris/Kigali 2004, pp. 24f.

147 See Marc Sommers/Elizabeth McClintock: On Hidden Ground. One Coexistence Strategy in Central Africa, in: Antonia Chayes/Martha Minow (eds.): Imagine Coexistence. Restoring Humanity after Violent Ethnic Conflict, San Francisco et al. 2003, p. 37; Peter Uvin: Reading the Rwandan Genocide, in: International Studies Review, Vol. 3 (2001) 3, p. 78.

148 See Mamdani: From Conquest to Consent, p. 7.

149 See Mamdani: When Victims Become Killers, p. 74.

150 See Strizek: Kongo, Zaire – Ruanda – Burundi, p. 32.

151 See Strizek: Ruanda und Burundi von der Unabhängigkeit zum Staatszerfall, p. 38.

152 See Cyprian F. Fisiy: Of Journeys and Border Crossings, p. 20.

and poor, or exploited and exploiters.[153] Equally, clans consisted of Hutu and Tutsi, and even Twa, whereas families and lineages were mono-ethnic as children took on the ethnicity of the father.[154] But it can be regarded as a fact that Tutsi occupied the highest ranks in the social order of Rwanda and Hutu and Twa found themselves at the bottom of the strata, even if mobility existed in between.[155]

Transformations in the 19th century within the Rwandan state hardened the identities, but these changes first and foremost created a division between the king's court in the centre and the periphery, and not between Hutu and Tutsi. However, these changes were the beginning of modern society in Rwanda and gave birth to the problems that followed.[156] A division between a pastoralist aristocracy and a subject peasantry was created. Most of this peasantry was Hutu, even if the *petits Tutsi* had the same economic status as Hutu. Also, Hutu could become Tutsi, which prevented the development of a counter elite. What is vital here is that the Tutsi aristocracy developed a political conscience and saw themselves as superior to the subject masses.[157] "To be a Tutsi was thus to be in power, near power, or simply to be identified with power – just as to be Hutu was more and more to be a subject."[158] The complexity of the Rwandese society gave way to a division between powerful and powerless towards the end of the 19th century, and as each group belonged clearly to one side of the division, a political distinction was created that came to be associated with either group. It is therefore important to understand these developments to judge the discussion about Tutsi supremacy in Rwandese history. It is necessary to note, however, that Hutu and Tutsi have not

---

153 See Mamdani: When Victims Become Killers, p. 74.

154 See Prunier: The Rwanda Crisis, p. 15.

155 See Anne Mackintosh: Rwanda. Beyond Ethnic Conflict, in: Development in Practice, Vol. 7 (1997) 4, p. 471.

156 See Prunier: The Rwanda Crisis, p. 21. On pages 19-23 Prunier describes these transformations in detail.

157 See Mamdani: From Conquest to Consent, p. 8ff.
Two myths deal with the origin of the Rwandese people: The Gihanga-myth stresses that all groups in Rwanda share the same ancestor Gihanga and therefore live in unity. The youngest son of Gihanga (representing the Tutsi) had been the most talented and therefore the natural leader and ruler over the others. The other myth is more divisive. According to that Kigwa-myth there were three groups of different ancestry: one group came from heaven to earth, one is associated with earth and one descends from beneath the ground. As the Tutsi descended to earth it is clear that they must be the dominant and superior group. See Strizek: Ruanda und Burundi von der Unabhängigkeit zum Staatszerfall, p. 68.

158 Mamdani: When Victims Become Killers, p. 75.

been enemies for centuries and there was no systematic violence between the groups before independence.[159]

3.1.2 Colonial influence on perceptions of ethnicity

While the pre-colonial history of Rwanda is heavily disputed and fills libraries with different theories, the basic facts of the Belgian period are commonly agreed on.[160] The supremacy of the Tutsi oligarchy was strengthened by the Belgian colonizers as they opted to reign Rwanda through the king's court.[161] Arriving in Rwanda, the European explorers were struck by the existing physiognomic differences between the natives. As Hutu, Tutsi and Twa had different features, the race-obsessed Europeans of the early twentieth century concluded that they must belong to different races.[162] They ignored the complex structure of Rwandese society and erected a colonial bureaucracy tailored on their perception of Rwandese realities that explained Rwandese society so much better than the complex realities of history.[163] It was therefore the Belgians that helped the Tutsi to acquire all relevant positions and claim all chief titles for them.[164] And it was also the Belgians that introduced ethnic identity cards to easily identify which group a person belonged to.[165]

For the Europeans at the time it seemed impossible that the black race could create a state structure similar to European achievements and thus everything that resembled European genius must have come from outside of Africa. For this purpose they constructed the so-called Hamites that were said to be related to Anglo-Saxons and Germans.[166] Mahmood Mamdani gives an excellent

---

159 See Leonard Harding/Carsten Heeger: Versuch einer Erklärung. Eine theoretische Annäherung an den Völkermord, in: Leonard Harding (ed.): Ruanda – der Weg zum Völkermord. Vorgeschichte, Verlauf, Deutung, Hamburg 1998, p. 207; Prunier: The Rwanda Crisis, p. 39.

160 See Penal Reform International: From Camp to Hill, p. 25.

161 See Strizek: Ruanda und Burundi von der Unabhängigkeit zum Staatszerfall, p. 39.

162 See Prunier: The Rwanda Crisis, pp. 6f.

163 See Carsten Heeger: Die Erfindung der Ethnien in der Kolonialzeit. „Am Anfang stand das Wort", in: Leonard Harding (ed.): Ruanda – der Weg zum Völkermord. Vorgeschichte, Verlauf, Deutung, Hamburg 1998, p. 26; Prunier: The Rwanda Crisis, p. 38.

164 See Theodor Hanf: Die politische Bedeutung ethnischer Gegensätze in Ruanda und Burundi, Freiburg 1964 (Materialien des Arnold Bergstraesser Instituts für Kulturwissenschaftliche Forschung), p. 23.

165 See Heeger: Die Erfindung der Ethnien in der Kolonialzeit, p. 29.

166 See Heeger: Die Erfindung der Ethnien in der Kolonialzeit, p. 21.
As Mamdani points out: The Hamitic hypothesis was not restricted to Rwanda, it was in fact used for many groups in Africa like the Hima in Baganda, but only in Rwanda and Burundi it fixed the Tutsi as an alien race as opposed to an ethnic group. See Mamdani: When Victims Become Killers, p. 35.

explanation of how the foundation for future conflict was laid by the colonizers. The dialectic of native and settler, initially used to differentiate between the colonizers and the indigenous population in Africa, was also used in constructing Hutu as indigenous Bantu and Tutsi as foreign Hamites. In order to understand that mechanism one has to explore the use of direct and indirect colonial rule. Direct rule divided society along racial lines into the superior settler and the inferior native. But this division proved to be a serious problem and made for a crisis of direct rule as the subjects were able to organize themselves as one racial group, much more numerous than the settler group and therefore potentially dangerous to their hold on power. This is why the colonized majority had to be divided into several political minorities. To achieve this, ethnicity was introduced. Thus the colonizers created two kinds of divisions: the first between settler and native (racial) and the second among the natives (ethnic). Ethnicity was therefore an internal, horizontal division while race marked an external, vertical division. Yet only "natives" in the colonies belonged to ethnic groups, non-natives were regarded as a different race. The colonizers in fact created a division between two kinds of colonized: indigenous and alien. By constructing one colonized group as non-indigenous as opposed to the indigenous natives it created a space between settler and native that could be filled by a so-called subject race that was also non-indigenous. Throughout Africa such non-indigenous subject races have been constructed on purpose by the colonizers to fill the middle ground between settler and native: the Arabs of Zanzibar, the Coloureds in South Africa, the Asians in East Africa and the Tutsi in Rwanda. They were, although Africans, constructed as foreigners as opposed to indigenous Bantu.[167] This construction was later used to label Tutsi as alien invaders that needed to be eliminated.
The racism of the colonizers had a profound impact on Hutu and Tutsi. Tutsi developed feelings of superiority and regarded themselves as meant to rule. Hutu conscience, on the other hand, was crushed, and a massive inferiority complex developed that heavily influenced politics after the Belgians had left. Gérard Prunier calls this process the manufacturing of a social bomb waiting to explode.[168] The time for that first explosion came on the eve of independence, when the formerly accepted social system began to change and Hutu and Tutsi began to mend the Belgian perceptions into their own belief systems and used the newly created social space to enter the political arena with

167 See Mamdani: When Victims Become Killers, pp. 25ff.

168 See Prunier: The Rwanda Crisis, pp. 9 and 28.

exactly the same ethnic and racial stereotypes the colonizers had inflicted on them.[169]

3.1.3 Developments after independence

Leonard Harding and Carsten Heeger describe the situation after independence as a classic blueprint for politicized ethnicity. Instead of opposing parties with political programmes two peoples opposed each other that had no intentions to share power and identified themselves as rulers and ruled respectively.[170] When Rwanda was about to gain independence the Tutsi naturally demanded power for them. But once more the colonial politics influenced the power balance in Rwanda when the colonizers shifted their support to the Hutu who they thought could be manipulated more easily. This profoundly altered the situation and changed structures that had existed for centuries.[171]
The first post-independence Hutu president of Rwanda, Gregoire Kayibanda, defined Hutu and Tutsi as two separate nations that had no attachment to each other and could well be deemed inhabitants of different planets.[172] He drew on the identities developed by the colonizers and pursued a racialized nationalism that excluded a concept of unified citizenship as developed under Julius Nyerere in Tanzania. Hutu and Tutsi as bipolar racial identities were cast in stone by post-independence politics.[173]
Hutu intellectuals had portrayed the conflict in the beginning as one between classes, and between haves and have-nots, and thus called for freedom from an oppressive feudalist monarchy.[174] But increasingly Hutu politicians and the fraction of "Hutu Power" in particular, drew on ethnic and racial arguments to underscore their claim for power. They concluded that it was not the Europeans who sew division between Hutu and Tutsi in Rwanda, but that ethnic groups had existed before, and that the minority Tutsi group had always deprived the Hutu majority of their right to rule.[175] The Hutu Manifest of 1957 made clear that the Tutsi had an unjustified political monopoly that also gave them the lion's share of economic wealth. But most importantly, it claimed that the Tutsi were another race, and by taking over the racist notion

169 See Eva Rink/Wolfgang Schreiber: Die Entdeckung von Ethnizität und die Bildung politischer Parteien, in: Leonard Harding (ed.): Ruanda – der Weg zum Völkermord. Vorgeschichte, Verlauf, Deutung, Hamburg 1998, p. 48.

170 See Harding/Heeger: Versuch einer Erklärung, p. 209.

171 See Lunn: The African Great Lakes Region, p. 37.

172 See Ian S. Spears: Understanding Inclusive Peace Agreements in Africa. The Problems of Sharing Power, in: Third World Quarterly, Vol. 21 (2000) 1, p. 109.

173 See Mamdani: When Victims Become Killers, pp. 32 and 35.

174 See Hanf: Die politische Bedeutung ethnischer Gegensätze in Ruanda und Burundi, p. 18.

175 See Strizek: Ruanda und Burundi von der Unabhängigkeit zum Staatszerfall, p. 72.

of the colonial power it drew a division that was impossible to overcome thereafter.[176]

Through independence Hutu gained a monopoly on power and they made sure they would not lose it again. Whenever they feared a Tutsi conspiracy to take back power, massacres and killings were used to defend it.[177] Regional developments played a role, and so the 1972 genocide of Hutu by Tutsi in Burundi sparked anti-Tutsi violence in Rwanda as it was proven once more for Hutu that the Tutsi would do about anything to regain power and had to be prevented from doing so by violent means.[178] To conclude: the 1959 revolution of Hutu built on the racialized system of the Belgians, and demanded justice for the Hutu majority. This justice was then turned into revenge more and more, and frequent violence was the consequence. Only the second republic under president Habyarimana changed the status of the Tutsi from race to ethnicity, which gave them a status as an ethnic minority and no longer that of an alien race.[179]

3.1.4 The genocide and its impact on perceptions of ethnicity

In conflict situations internal group cohesion is usually achieved through an enemy image and the perceived threat that this enemy poses for the in-group. The threat is generally regarded as even more dangerous when violence and distrust are deeply rooted in the history of the warring parties as in Rwanda.[180] In Rwanda, leaders made sure to achieve that internal cohesion by making Hutu believe that Tutsi were another racial group, potentially dangerous as they longed for power and would take it from Hutu. The propaganda of the regime made people believe that this was an ethnic conflict.[181] This paper argues, however, that ethnic and racial categories are confused in this case. Drawing on Mahmood Mamdani this thesis suggests that indeed the Tutsi were not marked as an ethnic group but as an alien racial group. This group, being alien in their presence in Rwanda, could be wiped out with an easy conscience. Ethnic violence, Mamdani argues, can lead to excesses and massacres, but only thinking in racial terms can lead to genocide: to the extermination of

---

176 See Rink/Schreiber: Die Entdeckung von Ethnizität und die Bildung politischer Parteien, pp. 50f.

177 See Fisiy: Of Journeys and Border Crossings, p. 21.

178 See Lemarchand: Genocide in the Great Lakes, p. 6.

179 See Mamdani: When Victims Become Killers, p. 16.

180 See Lederach: Building Peace, p. 13.

181 See Joshua G. Smith: Fighting Fear. Exploring the Dynamic Between Security Concerns and Elite Manipulation in Internal Conflict, in: Peace, Conflict and Development, Vol. 8 (2006) 8, in: http://www.peacestudiesjournal.org.uk/docs/Feb%2006%20SMITH.pdf (15.03.2008), p. 25.

another people. The term "ethnic" needs to be used with that background in mind.[182] This view is supported by Leonard Harding who states that all Tutsi were regarded as enemies of the Hutu state and were suspected of collaborating with the RPF invasion. They thus belonged to that outside group that wanted to conquer Rwanda, and were not regarded as citizens of the Rwandan state, which should be a Hutu state exclusively.[183]

The civil war led to a radicalization of both groups. The immediate threat successfully created enemy images and the other group became a synonym for evil and destruction.[184] Hutu believed they were doing good by killing Tutsi. Ethnicity became a matter of "us and them", where the own group was viewed as good in opposition to the evil others.[185] Ethnicity and the feeling of belonging to one particular group had been internalized by Rwandans since the colonial period (or perhaps even earlier). But the war and genocide inflated these feelings enormously and created a division deeper than anytime in history.[186]

It is also important to bear in mind that every Rwandan has been affected by the genocide and the violence that followed it in one or the other way. The experience of extreme violence is likely to have hardened identities that existed before.[187] As the Rwanda crisis can be described as an intractable conflict with violent outbursts over generations and perceived as a zero-sum game, the genocide played on existing stereotypes and deepened divisions by its ultraviolence.[188] This leads Anne Mackintosh to conclude: "Whether or not it was truly so before, 'ethnicity' has become a key factor"[189] through the genocide and the division is deeper now than ever before. Mahmood Mamdani claims that the genocide left "tensions that are volcanic in nature"[190] in Rwandese society.

---

182 See Mamdani: When Victims Become Killers, pp. 13f.

183 See Harding/Heeger: Versuch einer Erklärung, p. 214.

184 See Matthias Hufmann: Die Verunsicherung von außen und der Aufbau eines neuen Feindbildes, in: Leonard Harding (ed.): Ruanda – der Weg zum Völkermord. Vorgeschichte, Verlauf, Deutung, Hamburg 1998, p. 103.

185 See Maogoto: The International Criminal Tribunal for Rwanda, p. 66.

186 See Penal Reform International: From Camp to Hill, p. 38.

187 See Joel Nsengiyaremye: Zehn Jahre danach. Völkermord in Ruanda, in: Jörg Calliess (ed.): Zehn Jahre danach. Völkermord in Ruanda, Loccum 2005 (Dokumentation einer Tagung der evangelischen Akademie Loccum vom 5. bis 7. März 2004), p. 92.

188 See Brounéus: Reconciliation. Theory and Practice for Development Cooperation, p. 49.

189 Mackintosh: Rwanda. Beyond Ethnic Conflict, p. 470.

190 Mamdani: When Victims Become Killers, p. 265.

It also shaped political and military thinking by the new regime, as the experience of genocide laid like a shadow over every decision taken.[191] Furthermore, it influenced the perception of history profoundly and determined what is being remembered or forgotten by the opposing groups.[192] Tales of victimization strengthen group identity within ethnic groups and this has certainly been the case in Rwanda. The experience of violence also leads to the creation of myths that influence the perception of group members for generations to come. Experts call traumatic events that are glorified and retold within a group *chosen trauma*.[193] Hutu and Tutsi have developed several myths and *chosen traumata* that will be analyzed in the next chapter.

3.2 The interpretation of history along ethnic lines: Myths and *chosen trauma*

It is important to lay out the known facts about the history of Rwanda and the creation of ethnicity, as well as the impact of the genocide in fixing ethnic identities. It is equally important, however, to assess the different interpretations of history that play a significant role in Rwanda today. What people believe has happened can be very distinct from what actually happened, but is equally important for the reconciliation process.[194]

The same events are perceived and interpreted radically different by Hutu and Tutsi. René Lemarchand points out that these different cognitive maps have always provided justification for further violence. It is not uncommon for Hutu to contest that the 1994 genocide ever happened. In that view massacres did occur, but were sparked by the RPF invasion and a consequence of the civil war, not carefully planned genocidal killing. This suggests that the RPF bears the guilt for the 1994 events.[195] Some even go so far to claim that, while everyone was killing, Hutu were the main victims and the casualties among the Tutsi far less in number than those among Hutu.[196] Another myth circulating is the "double genocide theory" which claims that the killings of refugees in the DRC camps in the years after the genocide constituted a second genocide, committed by the victorious RPF forces against Hutu.[197] Denial of the geno-

---

191 See Elizabeth Sidiropoulos: Democratisation and Militarisation in Rwanda. Eight Years After the Genocide, in: African Security Review, Vol. 11 (2002) 3, in: http://www.iss.co.za/ASR/11No3/Sidiropoulos.html (10.01.2008), [Subsection 1].

192 See Lemarchand: Genocide in the Great Lakes, p. 7.

193 See Barsalou: Trauma and Transitional Justice in Divided Societies, p. 4.

194 See Bloomfield: The Context of Reconciliation, p. 40.

195 See Lemarchand: Genocide in the Great Lakes, pp. 5 and 7.

196 See Jeremy Sarkin: The Tension Between Justice and Reconciliation in Rwanda. Politics, Human Rights, Due Process and the Role of the Gacaca Courts in Dealing With the Genocide, in: Journal of African Law, Vol. 45 (2001) 2, p. 150.

197 See International Crisis Group: Rwanda at the End of the Transition, p. 27.

cide was facilitated by the fact that militia and former Rwandese army elements controlled the refugee camps in neighbouring countries very tightly. Exposed to genocidal propaganda in the camps, the lack of remorse by Hutu is not very surprising.[198] With all these myths circulating it is clear that there is little truth about the 1994 events in Rwanda that is commonly agreed on.[199] Consequently, the lack of a shared account of the past makes a decision on how to deal with that past and reconcile perpetrators and victims all the more difficult, as the line between them becomes blurred.[200]

But not only the genocide is a contested issue, the history of Rwanda usually comes in two versions, too. The RPF view claims that Belgian colonial administration created ethnic divisions that later led to the genocide. Following this narrative the year 1959 did not mark a revolution as claimed by the Hutu, but the first genocide in Rwanda.[201] A popular RPF song states that Rwandans had been living in unity before colonization, and can regain this unity now. In the last consequence this suggests that the white man bears the guilt of genocide and massacres, not the Rwandans themselves.[202] This view also holds that the Tutsi were established as the privileged group by the Belgians. Hutu instead claim that Tutsi privilege and exploitation of Hutu in feudal structures have existed in Rwanda long before the colonizers arrived.[203] For Hutu, generally speaking, the Tutsi king has suppressed Hutu and Twa by means of forced labour. This discrimination existed in pre-colonial times and paved the way for future discrimination. It is also common to regard Tutsi as vicious and clever, a people that cannot be trusted.[204] A telling example of these conflicting views is the ancient institution of *ubuhake*.[205] Tutsi later claimed it was a favourable institution that helped Hutu to gain economic success; Hutu dis-

198 See Prunier: The Rwanda Crisis, p. 315.

199 See Drumbl: Punishment, Postgenocide, p. 1270.

200 See Mark R. Amstutz: Is Reconciliation Possible After Genocide? The Case of Rwanda, in: Journal of Church and State, Vol. 48 (2006) 3, p. 548.

201 See Timothy Longman/Théonèste Rutagengwa: Memory, Identity and Community in Rwanda, in: Eric Stover et al. (eds.): My Neighbour, My Enemy. Justice and Community in the Aftermath of Mass Atrocity, Cambridge 2004, p. 165.

202 See Des Forges: Leave None to Tell the Story, p. 693.

203 See Mamdani: When Victims Become Killers, p. 269.

204 See Corey/Joireman: Retributive Justice, p. 76.

205 The *ubuhake* is a form of clientship where two men enter an unequal contract. The Tutsi patron usually gave a cow to its cattle less Hutu client. The calves of that cow would then be shared between the patron and client. This institution could provide a possibility for Hutu to become tutsified. But if the patron demanded too many social and economic obligations from the client the deal did not provide any advantages for the client. See Prunier: The Rwanda Crisis, p. 13.

missed it as a form of exploitation similar to slavery that was used to suppress Hutu.[206]

These views differ substantially from each other and can be defined as selective memories that are usually transferred from one generation to the next and thus create diverging histories championed by each group.[207] Subjective narratives about oppression and past victimization keep the cycle of mistrust towards the other group alive. Furthermore they legitimize the use of violence against this group in the present, especially when the in-group is perceived to be under substantial threat. This process in Rwanda's case served as a legitimization for the genocide as well as reprisal killings by the RPF after the end of the war.[208] As killings justified by past victimization always lead to new reprisals by the newly victimized group, the vicious cycles of violence are kept alive and people on both sides of the divide learn to hate the other group for what it has done to the own group in the past.[209] Experience in Bosnia has shown that each group of the conflict presents itself as victims and consequently no group is interested in investigating the atrocities committed by the own group.[210] The same holds true for Rwanda where the dominant narrative among the Hutu group claims that they were the real victims of Tutsi quest for power and influence.[211] This view leads to the denial of the genocide as portrayed before.

The most problematic aspect of these dominant selective narratives is the fact that the longer these beliefs have been kept vivid the more difficult it is to overcome them and form a new, uniting history. But abandoning these narratives in favour of a shared account of the past where suffering of both groups is equally recognized and the stories of victimization are transformed into narratives of empowerment is a prerequisite for reconciliation.[212] Solely dismissing the other narratives (of the Hutu) as rumours that confuse the population is not going to help in this regard.[213] Instead, René Lemarchand is right when he claims that

"unless a concerted effort is made to get closer to the facts and move out of the fantasy-land of official mythologies, the collective memory of Hutu and

---

206 See Prunier: The Rwanda Crisis, p. 13.

207 See Huyse: The Process of Reconciliation, p. 30.

208 See Wohl/Branscombe: Forgiving the Ingroup or the Outgroup for Harm Doing, p. 19.

209 See Mackintosh: Rwanda. Beyond Ethnic Conflict, p. 471.

210 See Fletcher/Weinstein: Violence and Social Repair, p. 589.

211 See Des Forges: Leave None to Tell the Story, p. 81.

212 See Sluzki: The Process Toward Reconciliation, p. 29.

213 See NURC/GTZ: NURC-GTZ Conference on the Presentation of the Grassroots Consultation and Evaluation Report. Kigali, Hotel des Milles Collines 25th of July 2002, Kigali 2002, in: www.grandlacs.net/doc/2968.pdf (10.02.2008), p. 7.

Tutsi will continue to enshrine the same myths, with little hope in sight that the killing may stop."[214]

The search for truth, crucially important for reconciliation as we have seen in chapter 2, therefore needs to take these myths and narratives into account. They are enshrined in the memories of both groups and objective facts about the history of Rwanda will probably not help to establish truth about victimization unless these myths are considered to be part of history. If it is true, as Gérard Prunier states, that "Hutu and Tutsi have killed each other more to upbraid a certain vision they have of themselves, of the others and of their place in the world than because of material interests"[215], including these narratives in the reconciliation process is an absolute necessity.

3.3 Ethnicity in Rwanda today

3.3.1 Cleavages in modern Rwandese society

After the genocide and the establishment of a new regime in Rwanda several social cleavages can be identified that are not only of ethnic character but also include regional, socio-economic and political factors. Hofmeier identifies nine different groups in contemporary Rwanda. First, there are Tutsi survivors of the genocide, known as *rescapés*, as opposed to the Tutsi returnees that have hardly been affected by the genocide themselves. Another group of mainly Tutsi are the ruling elite of president Kagame that are less interested in ethnic affiliations but in securing the Rwandan state from outside threats. The majority in Rwanda consists of Hutu peasants that have never left the country and usually don't interpret tensions as ethnic. Furthermore, there are the so-called second caseload refugees[216], Hutu that fled to the neighbouring countries (mainly the DRC) after the genocide and have brought back strong resentments against Tutsi from living in the refugee camps abroad. Two other Hutu groups can be identified, namely the Hutu in public office, who distance themselves from ethnic thinking, and the exiled Hutu that left Rwanda because of tensions with the ruling RPF. Only the rebel groups in the DRC that consist of former militias are pursuing an armed struggle against the government. Parts of the Rwandan army RPA make up another group that is known for their negative attitude towards Hutu as a result of long years of war. The

---

214 See Lemarchand: Genocide in the Great Lakes, p. 14.

215 See Prunier: The Rwanda Crisis, p. 40.

216 The first caseload refugees are the Tutsi that fled anti-Tutsi reprisals in the first and second republic from 1959 onwards and settled in neighbouring states. Their children make up the biggest part of the returnees.

last group Hofmeier includes in his analysis are the foreign diplomats, experts and development workers.[217]

The Tutsi group, however, is clearly split into the genocide survivors that stayed in the country in 1994 and the returnees that make up the political and economic elite of the country and look down upon the traumatized survivors who they regard as a relict of the past.[218] But the returnees are also split into various groups depending on their country of refuge. Each group carries nicknames and can thus easily be distinguished from other returnees: "Waragi" (which is a popular Ugandan liquor) or "left-hand drivers" are the returnees from Uganda, the Congolose carry the "Dubai label" and the Burundese are named "G.P." after the presidential guard in Burundi.[219] Tensions have been growing between the different diasporas as the Ugandans make up the inner power circle of government and Burundese and Congolose returnees feel excluded from power, wealth and the highest ranks of the military.[220] The picture of Rwandese society is therefore not as clear as one might think regarding the ethnic roots of the conflict.

Mamdani puts a different emphasis in his analysis of the existing groups in Rwanda today that highlights the ethnic components of the terms used by Hofmeier and in Rwandan politics – and the presumed involvement in the genocide. He supposes five categories, namely the returnees, refugees, victims, survivors and perpetrators. While the returnees are mainly Tutsi and few Hutu exiles that returned after the genocide with the RPF, the refugees are made up of old caseload (Tutsi pre-genocide refugees) and new caseload refugees (Hutu post-genocide refugees). Victims can be both Hutu and Tutsi while living victims can be only first caseload refugees and Tutsi genocide survivors, not new caseload refugees. Survivors are only Tutsi as the genocide was aimed at eliminating only that group. The logical consequence is that the last group, the perpetrators, consists only of Hutu, and as moderate Hutu are believed to have been killed in the genocide every living Hutu is presumed to be a perpetrator.[221]

As can be seen, the terms used by Hofmeier and Mamdani can be applied to different groups and one person in Rwanda can be a member of different groups at the same time. Indeed there exist so many different sub-groups in Rwanda now that even Rwandans have difficulties to name them all. Philip Gourevitch describes the overlapping of these segments with several markers

217 See Hofmeier: Soziokulturelle Kurzanalyse Ruanda, pp. 5f.

218 See Colette Braeckmann: Rwanda. The Challenges After Victory, in: African Geopolitics, Vol. 13 (2004), in: http://www.african-geopolitics.org/home_english.htm (12.01.2008), [Subsection 5].

219 See Sommers/McClintock: On Hidden Ground, p. 40.

220 See International Crisis Group: Rwanda at the End of the Transition, p. 18.

221 See Mamdani: When Vicims Become Killers, p. 267.

such as ethnicity, regional provenance, exile backgrounds, RPF affiliation or opposition, attitude towards other political tendencies such as Hutu Power, clans or religion.[222] These subgroups have potentially similar interests that could bridge the all powerful divide of ethnicity.[223] However, it seems that a repetition of the colonial pattern is likely to keep up ethnic affiliation as a stronger marker than identification with a sub-group of society. While Hutu are engaged in subsistence farming, power and wealth are accumulated in the urban centres and within the Tutsi group. Tensions between different Tutsi groups exist but are likely to be overlooked by Hutu who feel excluded from wealth and influence once more. This perception sharpens ethnic differences and can bare grounds for violence.[224] Indeed, intermarriage between Hutu and Tutsi now causes great problems. The two groups frequently intermarried before the genocide but today parents often disapprove and do not support the couple. This is a strong indication for ongoing ethnic conflict.[225]

3.3.2 The ideology of national unity

The RPF has emphasized national unity as an important goal ever since the genocide began and tried to point out the political causes for the genocide as opposed to ethnic arguments.[226] It has employed the concept of "Rwandanness" that tries to eliminate ethnicity and other divisive factors all together to create a new and unified identity among Rwandan citizens.[227] The use of the terms Hutu and Tutsi is strongly discouraged by the government and people rarely employ them as a consequence.[228] Despite the political abuse of the RPF ideology and the ban of ethnic terms the sincerity of the RPF leadership in its quest for unity is not questioned here. The concept of "Rwandanness" was developed among the refugees in Uganda as they felt increasing discrimination on behalf of native Ugandans. While they had tried to adapt to Ugan-

---

222 See Philip Gourevitch: Wir möchten Ihnen mitteilen, daß wir morgen mit unseren Familien umgebracht werden. Berichte aus Ruanda, Berlin 1999, p. 277.

223 See Bloomfield: The Context of Reconciliation, p. 45.

224 See Sarkin: The Necessity and Challenges of Establishing a Truth and Reconciliation Commission in Rwanda, p. 786.

225 See Rosemarie McNairn: Building Capacity to Resolve Conflict in Communities. Oxfam Experience in Rwanda, in: Gender and Development, Vol. 12 (2004) 3, p. 87.

226 See Des Forges: Leave None to Tell the Story, p. 694.

227 See Amstutz: Is Reconciliation Possible After Genocide?, p. 547.

228 See Gubin/Hagengimana/Pearlman/Staub: Healing, Reconciliation, Forgiving and the Prevention of Violence After Genocide or Mass Killing, p. 315. This view is underscored by personal observations of the author in Rwanda.

dan society, the hostility by and exclusion from that society strengthened their identity as Banyarwanda rather than Tutsi.[229]
National unity and ending ethnic antagonism is a worthwhile goal, and the creation of new identity cards without reference to ethnic groups a necessary consequence in light of the role these cards played in identifying Tutsi to be killed in the genocide. But banning of ethnicity can hinder the healing process in Rwanda.[230] If talk about the genocide is permitted and vivid in political and social life, restricting discussions on ethnicity are likely to aggravate conflict. Ethnicity just lingers under the surface and will emerge again, with violence being its potential companion.[231] In fact, it can be observed that Rwandans do not embrace the government's rhetoric and ethnic divisions continue to exist.[232] One example for this is the fact that Hutu and Tutsi do not visit the same bars in Kigali, which strengthens distrust and the development of rumours.[233] Another is the harassment of Tutsi genocide survivors in Rwandan schools by their fellow Hutu students, which is believed to be a consequence of ethnic hatred still being taught at home and by some teachers.[234]
Rwandans easily identify Hutu and Tutsi in daily life, even if the terms are not used openly anymore. Even members of the elite, who embrace the concept of "Rwandanness" in official statements, do not hesitate to point out members of the different groups on the street.[235] "Rwandanness" possibly means nothing to the Rwandese people. They still identify strongly with their own ethnic group, probably even more than before the genocide. The personal attachment to ethnicity, however, is not necessarily damaging for reconciliation. Its abuse by the ruling elite has triggered violent conflict throughout the history of Rwanda. Therefore the RPF would do better by creating the grounds for a Rwandan citizenship that is not bound on ethnicity as under the genocidal regime, but provides independent institutions for all citizens. Banning of

229 See Mamdani: From Conquest to Consent, p. 25.
230 See Cynthia Burns/Laura McGrew/Ilija Todorovic: Imagine Coexistence Pilot Projects in Rwanda and Bosnia, in: Antonia Chayes/Martha Minow (eds.): Imagine Coexistence. Restoring Humanity after Violent Ethnic Conflict, San Francisco et al. 2003, p. 89.
231 See Sommers/McClintock: On Hidden Ground, p. 41.
232 See Tiemessen: After Arusha, p. 65.
233 See International Crisis Group: Rwanda at the End of the Transition, p. 17.
234 See Robert Walker: Genocide Hatred Lingers in Rwanda Schools, in: BBC News (19.02.2008), in: http://news.bbc.co.uk/go/pr/fr/-/2/hi/africa/7246985.stm (19.02.2008), [Subsection 2]; Robert Walker: Rwanda "Still Teaching Genocide" (17.01.2008), in: BBC News, in: http://news.bbc.co.uk/go/pr/fr/-/2/hi/africa/7194827.stm (18.01.2008), [Subsection 2].
235 See Hofmeier: Soziokulturelle Kurzanalyse Ruanda, p. 8; Mamdani: From Conquest to Consent, p. 5.

ethnicity is not necessary for these ends, and rather fruitless regarding the attitude of Rwandans towards ethnicity.[236]

There are two main problems with the RPF policy of national unity that endanger reconciliation in Rwanda. First, even though the concept aims at preventing conflict, it will probably aggravate tensions as ethnic issues and discrimination cannot be addressed.[237] Second, the inherent risk this policy poses is the presumption of national unity. As national unity is usually the outcome achieved by a successful reconciliation process, it is dangerous to assume that this unity already exists at the beginning of the endeavour.[238] The RPF therefore risks reconciliation and a united society when it suppresses ethnicity and rewrites history following its doctrine of a united country because "(...) deep down, each Rwandan identifies with a group."[239] Denial of this fact will not help to mend broken relationships between the groups.

236 See Drumbl: Punishment, Postgenocide, pp. 1294f.

237 See DED-ZFD: Strategische Planung des Zivilen Friedensdienstes in Ruanda 2007-2012, Kigali 2006, p. 1.

238 See Schilling: Gegen das Vergessen, p. 336.

239 Penal Reform International: From Camp to Hill, p. 41.

4 Dealing with the past and reconciliation in an authoritarian political climate

4.1 The domination of the reconciliation process by the RPF regime

Arriving at peace after violent conflict between opposing groups in a given state requires political measures aiming at reconciliation.[240] The RPF led government has identified four basic pillars it deems crucial for reconciliation: Addressing the myths circulating in Rwanda, punishing genocide crimes, rehabilitating and healing the victims and building a united country on the basis of a shared Rwandan identity.[241] Based on these pillars the government has initiated a series of programmes and policies. Apart from the judicial strategies dealing with the genocide that will be discussed later on, it has created re-education camps (the so-called *ingando*) to teach Rwandans about their history and the genocide, memorials have been erected all over the country and commemorations like a "National Day of Heroes" are held every year, especially in April. A new flag, anthem and national seal have been created to symbolize a new beginning and in 1999 and 2001 national and regional conferences on reconciliation have been held.[242] These policies constitute a second track in Rwanda's attempt to come to terms with the past. While courts try to establish what happened in 1994, the "National Unity and Reconciliation Commission" (NURC) is occupied with the reasons underlying the genocide.[243]

It has been argued that the NURC is an important model for reconciliation in post-conflict situations world wide as it shows the government's will to foster reconciliation.[244] On the other hand the NURC is far from being an independent reconciliation body or a truth commission and strongly dominated by government. This can very well limit its efficiency.[245] The NURC as well as other measures taken by the government towards reconciliation has serious

240 See Brounéus: Reconciliation. Theory and Practice for Development Cooperation, p. 25.

241 See Cobban: The Legacies of Collective Violence, [Subsection 5].

242 See Longman/Rutagengwa: Memory, Identity and Community in Rwanda, p. 166; Regina Wegemund: Nationale Aussöhnung in Ruanda. Chancen und Bedrohung, in: Internationales Afrikaforum, Vol. 38 (2002) 4, p. 368.

243 See Daly: Between Punitive and Reconstructive Justice, p. 358.

244 See Burns/McGrew/Todorovic: Imagine Coexistence Pilot Projects in Rwanda and Bosnia, p. 86.

245 See Sarkin: The Tension Between Justice and Reconciliation in Rwanda, p. 155.

weaknesses and the most worrying fact in that respect is the top-down manner in which these policies are carried out. The government assumes that Rwandans are as committed to reconciliation as the government[246] but in reality ordinary people are not asked what they suggest to make reconciliation work.[247]

In the eyes of the government keeping the memory of the genocide alive is an important part of the reconciliation policy. But this also means that the gruesome past is always present and continues to shape the life of Rwandans. Constant re-wakening of the past is counterproductive to healing wounds. Furthermore, it is highly problematic that only the genocide is remembered and acknowledged publicly while other atrocities committed during the civil war are swept under the carpet.[248] Memorials can foster reconciliation, but they can also achieve the contrary if they are politically abused and hold up certain reflections of history that are not shared by all groups of society.[249] The Rwandan government can choose how to remember the past, and it can leave out certain parts in an attempt to reshape public memory. But it will not be possible to influence collective memory completely and force the people to forget the myths and stories of victimization they have enshrined. Even if the RPF forgets, the affected population (mostly Hutu) will not forget that the genocide was followed by massacres committed by the RPF.[250] The government ignores that fact when it tries to impose a certain reading of the genocide and historical roots of the conflict upon the population through massive propaganda.[251] Part of that indoctrination happens in the *ingando*, where critical voices are absent and lectures only present the government's view according to Mgbako. Usually participants repeat these views afterwards, but if they really enshrine them or rather produce what they believe they should say is doubtful given the culture of obedience to authority in Rwanda.[252]

At present, the Hutu victims are not acknowledged in the official discourse of the genocide, and this selective memory influences society enormously.[253] It

---

246 See NURC/GTZ: NURC-GTZ Conference on the Presentation of the Grassroots Consultation and Evaluation Report, p. 12.

247 See Longman/Pham/Weinstein: Connecting Justice to Human Experience, p. 207.

248 See Huyse: The Process of Reconciliation, p. 30.

249 See Barsalou: Trauma and Transitional Justice in Divided Societies, p. 2.

250 See Forsberg: The Philosophy and Practice of Dealing With the Past, p. 69.

251 See Oomen: Donor-Driven Justice and its Discontents, p. 901.

252 See Chi Mgbako: Ingando Solidarity Camps. Reconciliation and Political Indoctrination in Post-Genocide Rwanda, in: Harvard Human Rights Journal, Vol. 18 (2005), in: http://www.law.harvard.edu/students/orgs/hrj/iss18/mgbako.pdf (23.03.2008), pp. 213f.

253 See Jennifer G. Riddell: Addressing Crimes Against International Law. Rwanda's Gacaca in Practice, Aberdeen 2005 (A Thesis Presented for the Degree of LL.M at the University of Aberdeen), p. 125.

leads to Hutu retreating from the reconciliation process as they view memorials and national commemorations as divisive. For many, commemorations are a Tutsi event where Hutu don't have a place and where their suffering is forgotten.[254] Furthermore, the government uses the genocide and its commemoration as a weapon in the political struggle. While grief is a Tutsi affair, the Hutu population carries the stigma of collective guilt. Rwanda is held hostage by the RPF by using the genocide as a justification for unjust policies and forcing the country to remember history through their interpretative lens. Civil society is widely excluded from the process even though such small grassroots efforts at reconciliation could provide a beacon of hope for Rwandese society.[255] Instead, president Kagame tries to build up an image as Rwanda's saviour who can prevent further violence and is the only political force dedicated to unity and reconciliation. This rules out efforts at the bottom of society and justifies the top-down approach.[256] However, if reconciliation is to work, efforts from above and below need to be combined and complement each other.[257] Change in attitudes and behaviour must be internalized by the people. If it is imposed by the government this change is not likely to last and conflict will reoccur.[258]

So far the RPF has successfully dominated the reconciliation discussion in Rwanda and imposed its reading of history on society. However, many Rwandans hold the opinion that obstacles to reconciliation lie within the ruling class rather than the ordinary peasants. It remains thus to be seen whether the imposition of an RPF dominated reconciliation will work.[259] If the government is truly committed to reconciliation, it should maybe opt for what Jean Elshtain calls "knowing forgetting". Rwanda needs to make a choice if the genocide is to shape the present completely, and thus divides the population into perpetrators and victims forever. Or if society decides to remember the past, just as Germans remember the Holocaust as an important part of their history, but does not hold an entire group accountable for years to come. This is currently happening in Rwanda and poses a serious obstacle for reconciliation.[260]

---

254 See Zorbas: Reconciliation in Post-genocide Rwanda, p. 40.

255 See Nsengiyaremye: Zehn Jahre danach, pp. 92f.

256 See Waugh: Paul Kagame and Rwanda, p. 194.

257 See Huyse: The Process of Reconciliation, p. 26.

258 See Assefa: The Meaning of Reconciliation, [Subsection 3].

259 See Longman/Rutagengwa: Memory, Identity and Community in Rwanda, p. 178.

260 See Elshtain: Politics and Forgiveness, pp. 48ff.

4.2 The authoritarian character of the RPF regime

4.2.1 The RPF as "Banyarwanda" and protector of all Tutsi

The genocide has led to the rule of "Tutsi Power" in Rwanda. This political ideology was shaped among Tutsi of the diaspora and feels responsible for the survival of all Tutsi globally.[261] Psychologically this view is explained by the direct and indirect traumatization of Tutsi in general, even if they were not present during the genocide. As the exiled Tutsi were not accepted in their respective country of refuge, they came to see themselves as Tutsi from Rwanda and thus feel victimized, too. So the returnees are very sensitive to perceived threats of violence against Tutsi and likely to retreat to self-defensive violence even if it is not necessary.[262] It is common for ethnic conflicts that the minority group feels threatened by a majority government that is believed to exclude them from power and wealth or to suppress them.[263] So the RPF prioritizes the survival of Tutsi over fair treatment of the Hutu population.[264]

But it is strongly felt by Rwandans that the ruling elite abuses the genocide to tighten their grip on power.[265] The RPF has taken over the victim issue to present itself as the protector of Tutsi, while it in fact uses the victims as a justification for their right to rule. This not only alienates the majority of Hutu, but also the victims themselves.[266] While the RPF enjoys support of Tutsi in general, some Tutsi and the *rescapés* in particular feel marginalized and therefore the main justification of the government appears to crumble.[267] The discontent of the *rescapés* goes so far to claim they have been sacrificed by the RPF in their quest to conquer Rwanda and the main goal of the invasion was not to save them but to gain power.[268]

In the end it is less important if the RPF is really dedicated to the victim issue or just abusing it. The central question asked by Mark Drumbl is: "Can the

261 See Mamdani: When Victims Become Killers, p. 18.

262 See Staub/Pearlman: Advancing Healing and Reconciliation, p. 215.

263 See Spengemann: Freedom's Hidden Price, p. 133.

264 See Thiemessen: After Arusha, p. 66.

265 See Longman/Rutagengwa: Memory, Identity and Community in Rwanda, p. 176.

266 See Luc Huyse: Victims, in: David Bloomfield/Teresa Barnes/Luc Huyse (eds.): Reconciliation After Violent Conflict. A Handbook, Stockholm 2003 (IDEA), in: http://www.idea.int/publications/reconciliation/upload/reconciliation_full.pdf (12.01.2008), p. 61.

267 See Hofmeier: Soziokulturelle Kurzanalyse Ruanda, pp. 9 and 22.

268 See International Crisis Group: Rwanda at the End of the Transition, p. 18. This claim is not unreasonable as Alison Des Forges has laid out in her detailed analysis of the genocide and civil war. See Des Forges: Leave None to Tell the Story, pp. 698ff.

RPF act both as the protector of all Tutsi everywhere and as the national government of the Rwandan people?"[269] Is it a democratic government for all Rwandans or an ethnocracy favouring the minority over the majority?

4.2.2 The slide towards authoritarianism

Democracy and public contestation are crucial for peace and reconciliation in Rwanda. Power must be equally distributed between the state and the population to avoid the risk of an all-powerful government resorting to violence in the future.[270] However, in Rwanda democracy poses a serious problem as a guilty majority and a fearful minority are facing each other in the same political framework and need to seek accommodation with the other group despite the obvious reservations the victimized minority might have.[271] This fear motivates the RPF government and is at the same time exploited by it to manipulate politics to its favour.[272]

While in the beginning the RPF displayed both openness and inclusiveness as well as violence and discrimination in its political conduct, it soon began to slide towards authoritarianism.[273] Helped by the genocide credit and a conspiracy of silence by the feelings of guilt of the international community, the RPF issued a number of amendments to the Arusha records that gave it a bigger share of power than originally envisioned and instituted a strong presidency.[274] An RPF friendly view holds that there were no decent political opponents to negotiate with for the victorious RPF, as the opposition was composed of "*genocidaires*" intended on taking back power.[275] The opposite side, as propagated by Helmut Strizek, claims that the RPF was in reality an aggressor force that interrupted the democratic transition process under way in Rwanda after the Arusha records.[276]

It can be regarded as a fact that the RPF killed widespread and systematically during the civil war and afterwards and that the victims were mostly civilian and Hutu. The atrocities were known to the command and, even if not ordered, tolerated by the RPF leaders.[277] The violent dissolution of a refugee

269 Drumbl: Punishment, Postgenocide, p. 1311.

270 See Wierzynska: Consolidating Democracy Through Rwanda's Transitional Gacaca Courts, pp. 1950f.

271 See Mamdani: When Victims Become Killers, p. 266.

272 See Smith: Fighting Fear, p. 4.

273 See Reynjens: Rwanda, Ten Years On, p. 179.

274 See Filip Reyntjens: Post-1994 Politics in Rwanda. Problematising "Liberation" and "Democratisation", in: Third World Quarterly, Vol. 27 (2006) 6, pp. 1103ff.

275 See Prunier: The Rwanda Crisis, p. 355.

276 See Strizek: Kongo, Zaire – Ruanda – Burundi, pp. 165 and 197.

277 See Des Forges: Leave None to Tell the Story, pp. 693 and 734.

camp in Kibeho in 1995 and the "Gersony Report"[278] made the denial of atrocities impossible and some RPF commanders were tried, usually for minor offences.[279] The extent of the violence committed by RPF forces remains contested. Prunier estimates that up to 650.000 Hutu were killed in massacres, violent dissolutions of refugee camps in the DRC and through the Rwandese involvement in the Congolese war after 1997.[280] If these figures were correct, talk of a second genocide committed by RPF troops against Hutu could not be dismissed as unsubstantial.[281] But as figures are weapons in a propaganda war and impossible to establish, these claims seem questionable. Far better documented is the infiltration by ex-militia operating from Congo into Rwanda that targeted especially genocide survivors and lent legitimacy to the RPF's military actions in the DRC and at home.[282]

These outside threats also gave the RPF the opportunity to pursue its fight against divisionism inside Rwanda. Divisionist activities are banned by the constitution and the RPF has the right to cut political freedoms to prevent such activities.[283] Certainly ethnicity can no longer serve as a fundament for politics after its grave abuse in the genocide. However, the line between banning ethnic divisionism and abusing the argument to mete out political opposition is thin.[284] Abuse is further facilitated by the fact that most parties in Rwanda still rely on ethnicity as a basic element for political affiliation.[285] Thus, criticism of the RPF and Kagame and questioning the ideology of national unity is denounced as divisionism and used to suppress the opposition.[286] Lists are drawn up to identify persons accused to carry divisionist attitudes.[287] The constant accusations of divisionism used to tighten the RPF's grip on power, however, contradict the claim that reconciliation has been brought about by the RPF policies and that the RPF is the only unifying force

---

278 An UNHCR team documented the systematic killings by the RPF but the report was later kept under wraps by the United Nations to avoid damage for the new regime and the UN itself. Parts of the report leaked to the public. See Des Forges: Leave None to Tell the Story, p. 726.

279 See Waugh: Paul Kagame and Rwanda, p. 151.

280 See Cobban: The Legacies of Collective Violence, [Subsection 7].

281 See Helmut Strizek: Zur Lage der Menschenrechte in Ruanda, p. 36.

282 See Stefan Siebels: Die Flüchtlingskrise, in: Leonard Harding (ed.): Ruanda – der Weg zum Völkermord. Vorgeschichte, Verlauf, Deutung, Hamburg 1998, p. 192.

283 See Hofmeier: Soziokulturelle Kurzanalyse Ruanda, p. 15.

284 See Waugh: Paul Kagame and Rwanda, pp. 203ff.

285 See Drumbl: Punishment, Postgenocide, p. 1302.

286 See Stroh: Legitimation allein durch Entwicklung?, p. 7.

287 Human Rights Watch: World Report 2007, New York et al. 2007, in: http://www.hrw.org/wr2k7/wr2007master.pdf (16.05.2007), p. 143.

in Rwanda. If reconciliation was really under way, divisionist attitudes should be on the decline rather than on the rise.[288]
The abuse of the divisionist argument is understandable from an RPF perspective as total control of society is a prerequisite for its survival as a minority party facing an electorate composed of a majority that belongs to another ethnic group.[289] On the other hand, the Arusha process and the following genocide deeply influenced the thinking of the current leaders and they undeniably believe that multi-party elections pose too great a risk to pursue early in Rwanda after the horrific atrocities of 1994. So the aim of the government is to change attitudes and beliefs of the population before they gain back their full political rights.[290] Given the Ugandan background of most of Rwanda's leading political personnel it is hardly astonishing that the RPF chose to follow the path of Uganda's president Yoweri Museveni that restricts party politics and pluralism. For the RPF, the Rwandan population first and foremost needed to be educated about the genocide and politics, rather than simply giving them the right to vote and risking to perpetuate the ethnic voting behaviour. Social rights are therefore to trump political rights.[291] There indeed exists a risk that early multi party elections and free political competition could lead to another violent form of Hutu majority rule. Given the history of Rwanda, the international community has so far accepted the argument of the RPF that unity and peace are threatened by unrestricted majority democracy.[292] The slaughter of Tutsi in 1994 therefore legitimizes the behaviour of the RPF and allows them to display themselves as victims, turning the genocide into an ideological weapon for the government.[293]
The attitude displayed by the RPF towards democracy is highly problematic, however. As much as their distrust of the population might be understandable, their self-perception as liberators of Rwanda coupled with a strong sense of moral rectitude leads them to believe that the Rwandan people are only truly prepared for democracy if they vote for the RPF, as it is the only party striving for unity and peace.[294] So the past is abused to establish a de-facto one-party-state, with other government parties being mere satellites of the

288 See Human Rights Watch: Killings in Eastern Rwanda. No 1, New York et al. 2007, in: http://www.hrw.org/backgrounder/africa/rwanda0107/rwanda0107web.pdf (16.05.2008), p. 13.
289 See Reyntjens: Post-1994 Politics in Rwanda, p. 1109.
290 See International Crisis Group: Rwanda at the End of the Transition, p. i.
291 See Waugh: Paul Kagame and Rwanda, pp. 161f.
292 See Stroh: Legitimation allein durch Entwicklung?, p. 7.
293 See Reyntjens: Rwanda, Ten Years On, p. 199.
294 See Longman/Rutagengwa: Memory, Identity and Community in Rwanda, p. 167.

RPF.[295] While the RPF enjoys impunity and justifies its actions with the moral compulsion to prevent another genocide, it can mete out political opposition with the argument of ethnic divisionism.[296]

Avoiding the pitfalls of ethnicity is a worthwhile goal. However, it has become obvious during the years of RPF rule that oppressing ethnicity serves to mask "Tutsification" of power. While this "Tutsification" could at first only be observed in economy and society, it is now even visible in government. The Hutu elite is excluded from power with the divisionist argument and only the Tutsi elite is seen as capable to govern the country. The ethnic composition of government cannot be addressed as the terms Hutu and Tutsi are banned, but is nevertheless an obvious fact to all Rwandans. Still, not only Hutu are excluded from power, but also Tutsi members of the RPF. Discontent is growing among RPF members as a small group of returnees enjoys privileges, political and military posts and wealth on the expense of the general population.[297] This small group of mainly Ugandan returnees, stemming from the period of the civil war against the Habyarimana government, makes up the inner circle of power around president Kagame and is regarded as a new form of *akazu*.[298]

When Fred Rwigema and Pasteur Bizimungu stepped down as prime minister and president in 2000 the real power of Paul Kagame became fully visible and the rift between Hutu and Tutsi and francophone and anglophone actors in the government was impossible to hide.[299] Bizimungu founded a new party in 2001 and was immediately put under house arrest.[300] Most of the Hutu leadership had already gone into exile from 1995 onwards as they became targets of harassment and killings. A second wave of exiles followed after the resigna-

295 See Robert Walker: Rwandans Still Divided 10 Years On (07.04.2004), in: BBC News, in: http://news.bbc.co.uk/go/pr/fr/-/2/hi/africa/3557565.stm (29.01.2008), [Subsection 4].

296 See Mamdani: When Victims Become Killers, p. 271.

297 See Reyntjens: Rwanda, Ten Years On, pp. 187ff.

298 See Sidiropoulos: Democratisation and Militarisation in Rwanda, [Subsection 3]. The *Akazu* was the inner power circle of the former Habyarimana regime, made up mainly of the clan of his wife Agathe Kaziga from the north of Rwanda. It infiltrated all echelons of the Rwandan state, especially the media and army, to maintain total control of society and politics. See: Olivia Saeger: The Importance of Political Elites. Comparative Case Study of South Africa and Rwanda, Haverford 2007, in: http://thesis.haverford.edu/dspace/bitstream/10066/1035/1/2007SaegerO.pdf (19.05.2008), pp. 18ff.

299 See Wegemund: Nationale Aussöhnung in Ruanda, p. 370.

300 See Reyntjens: Rwanda, Ten Years On, p. 193.
Bizimungu was later tried and sentenced to 15 years in prison. He was pardoned by president Kagame in April 2007. See Human Rights Watch: World Report 2007, p. 144; Human Rights Watch: World Report 2008, New York et al. 2008, in: http://hrw.org/wr2k8/pdfs/wr2k8_web.pdf (16.05.2008), p. 146.

tion of Bizimungu in 2000 and now also included Tutsi as a result of the growing tensions between returnees and survivors. Soon not only opposition but also high ranking RPF members left the country and the party. This is clear indication that Rwandans of all political and ethnic affiliation opposed the RPF system.[301] The RPF, being a successful insurgent movement with a strong sense of unity and clear chain of command, now saw this internal cohesion crumble. Khadiagala and Lyons assume that movements like the RPF usually do not tolerate political rivals and democratic structures. The same qualities that made the insurgency successful usually hinder the democratization process after the war is won.[302] This seems to hold true for the RPF, as the government responded to the departures and growing opposition with a further crackdown on opponents. From the outset pluralism has been a mere façade and compliance with the Arusha records was only superficial. A "Forum of Parties" can ban political parties without transparency.[303] The "Mouvement Démocratique Républicain" (MDR) that had been the most influential party besides the RPF experienced that fate in the run-up to the elections in 2003 on charges of divisionism. Earlier, the local elections in 2001 had followed the example of Ugandan politics where no parties are allowed and people can merely choose between different candidates without party affiliation. Those candidates were carefully chosen in the interests of the RPF.[304] Filip Reyntjens states that the local elections showed the first obvious signs of Rwanda's transformation into an RPF-state, where only members of the system acquired political posts. The national elections in 2003 only reinforced this perception. Campaigning was accompanied by intimidations and disappearances and observers noted fraud and manipulation during the election. Independent candidates were banned and parties hindered in their campaign. Paul Kagame was elected as president with an astonishing 95 percent approval. To sum up: The end of the transition in 2003 was marked by elections that can be described as a mere cosmetic exercise and an attempt to lend legitimacy to the rule of the RPF. Contrary to previous efforts the regime did not even try to hide its authoritarian rift anymore.[305] Kagame, who had already been the strong man behind the scenes as vice-president, now officially held all the power he had exercised secretly before. Until the elections the RPF had successfully upheld the façade of a consensual, multi-ethnic government.

301 See Reyntjens: Rwanda, Ten Years On, pp. 180ff.

302 See Gilbert M. Khadiagala/Terrence Lyons: The Challenges of Leadership in Post-Conflict Transitions. Lessons from Africa, in: Conflict Trends, (2006) 4, in: http://www.accord.org.za/ct/2006-4/CT4_2006_pg9-15.pdf (15.03.2008), pp. 10 and 15.

303 See International Crisis Group: Rwanda at the End of the Transition, p. 10.

304 See Hofmeier: Soziokulturelle Kurzanalyse Ruanda, p. 14.

305 See Reyntjens: Post-1994 Politics in Rwanda, pp. 1106ff.

From 2003 onwards Kagame became a repressive military dictator heading a minority regime, an image he had long tried to avoid.[306]

The authoritarian behaviour was not restricted to the political sphere, however. Civil society equally became a target of repression. Journalists were harassed and even violently attacked or imprisoned. Freedom of expression was limited and some journalists went into exile. NGOs faced restrictions, too, and many practiced self-censorship, as did the press.[307] Human rights organizations are especially in danger of being assaulted and intimidated. Even the survivor's organization Ibuka, an NGO that should be protected according to the official claim that the RPF speaks for survivors, saw its leaders attacked and replaced by RPF friendly activists. In general, civil society organizations are only tolerated if they do not challenge the official government view. Challenging the politicized justice system like Ibuka leads to severe consequences.[308] The RPF seems to underestimate that the lack of a vibrant and independent civil society is likely to lead to the formation of negative groupings that enforce divisionism instead of teaching people democratic values and behaviour.[309]

The repression of and control over the population is possible due to the enormous strength and influence of the army in Rwanda. Army and intelligence services are the basic pillars in the RPF's system of total control over its subjects.[310] Extreme militarization has characterized Rwanda since the early years of RPF rule when the army was the only functioning institution in the country and the immediate threat by ex-militia in the Congo allowed it to play an important role in Rwandan politics.[311] Intimidating the population by means of the military works all the better as obedience to authority has always been strong in Rwanda. Now again citizens, and Hutu in particular, do not feel free to speak their minds. The RPF, like the previous regime, is not creating a responsible and critical citizenry that could oppose future violence, but is instead reinforcing the culture of obedience that led to the genocide in the first place.[312]

The Rwandan polity can be described without reasonable doubt as a repressive authoritarian military regime following Stroh's assessment of the regime: Power is concentrated with the president and a small influential circle. Criticizing the president or the ruling RPF is a taboo, opposition parties, civil soci-

306 See Waugh: Paul Kagame and Rwanda, pp. 149 and 154.

307 See Amnesty International: World Report 2007, p. 220; Human Rights Watch: World Report 2007, pp. 144f.

308 See International Crisis Group: Rwanda at the End of the Transition, pp. 12f.

309 See Saeger: The Importance of Political Elites, p. 10.

310 See Reyntjens: Post-1994 Politics in Rwanda, p. 1110.

311 See Sidiropoulos: Democratisation and Militarisation in Rwanda, [Subsection 2].

312 See Longman/Rutagengwa: Memory, Identity and Community in Rwanda, p. 177.

ety and press are being sidelined or muzzled.[313] The RPF exercises total control over Rwanda through its intelligence and army capacity. It dominates the discourse on Rwanda's past, present and future through re-education camps and propaganda. In fact, critics of the government like Filip Reyntjens are of the opinion that one dictatorship has been replaced by another.[314] As the International Crisis Group states, "the RPF's ideology and the persistent security problems have locked the transition into an authoritarian drift, undermining all efforts at reconciliation in the short term and undermining the country's stability in the long term."[315]

4.3 Military dictatorship and ethnocracy in Rwanda and the implications for reconciliation: Can minority rule bridge the ethnic divide?

The underlying problems of Rwanda's transition to democracy are the irreconcilable views minority and majority have on that issue. While the survivors demand justice, the Hutu majority demands majority rule. For them pursuing justice is strengthening minority Tutsi rule, for Tutsi democracy is feared to lead to genocide again.[316] Understandable as these reservations might be, the need for democracy as a base for reconciliation is widely acknowledged. If one side does not accept this need for democracy – in Rwanda's case the victorious RPF after the civil war – reconciliation remains hollow.[317] If the transition is initiated by the complete victory of one party as in Rwanda's case, resentments and anger will likely linger under the surface, boiling secretly until the time for an explosion is ripe. Renewed violence is an almost certain outcome in these cases.[318]

Rwandans today know that the government is denying them political and civil rights and are frustrated by their continued exclusion from politics and wealth. Anger, frustration and desperation provide fertile grounds for violence to return.[319] These feelings are most strongly felt by the Hutu community, as they are collectively stigmatized as perpetrators of the genocide by the regime. Collective guilt is placed on the Hutu as a group.[320] In interviews renowned Rwanda experts Filip Reyntjens and Gérard Prunier claim that the Rwandan

---

313 See Stroh: Legitimation allein durch Entwicklung?, p. 6.
314 See Reyntjens: Post-1994 Politics in Rwanda, p. 1114.
315 International Crisis Group: Rwanda at the End of the Transition, p. 9.
316 See Mamdani: When Victims Become Killers, p. 274.
317 See Huyse: The Process of Reconciliation, p. 21.
318 See Bloomfield: The Context of Reconciliation, p. 43.
319 See Reyntjens: Rwanda, Ten Years On, p. 210.
320 See Zorbas: Reconciliation in Post-genocide Rwanda, p. 47.

government is holding the entire Hutu population as political hostages.[321] Hutu have been excluded from politics and the economy since the genocide. Especially second case-load refugees have been subjects of harassment after their return to Rwanda and reintegration seems difficult.[322] In the course of the new villagization policy of the government the population is resettled forcefully by the authorities into newly created villages. For the most part, these villages are inhabited by one ethnic group only and Hutu usually receive less assistance and resources than Tutsi.[323] As Hutu feel exclusion and disadvantages in daily life and have no possibility to voice criticism it is generally feared that resentments of that group will lead to future violence.[324] Former president Bizimungu is convinced that Hutu will prepare for war if the situation does not change, and that violence is unavoidable.[325] It does perhaps not astonish that genocide denial and rejection of guilt is growing in the Hutu community. The Hutu elite feels humiliated by the government, and repression and RPF atrocities reinforce ethnic thinking and partisan ethnic explanations of the genocide. These explanations are only brought forward privately, as voicing them in public would lead to imprisonment or death. But nevertheless different opinions circulate and are even more dangerous in their secret character than open contestation of the government view would be.[326] While Rwandans repeat the official propaganda of the RPF during the day, resentment is voiced behind closed doors during the night. The stability and peace Rwanda enjoys today are wallpapers pampering over cleavages. In fact, behaviour of people today resembles their behaviour before the genocide.[327]
Simultaneously, the behaviour of the government mirrors the pre-genocide regime. Not only Hutu are dissatisfied and make secret plans to overthrow the regime, the survivors are suspicious of the government, too, as they feel the RPF has sacrificed them to gain power. Both groups feel that the government only uses ethnicity to remain in power and that violent means are used to achieve this end.[328] This violence, committed by the RPA, is felt to target Hutu explicitly, and this view is strengthened by the fact that the army is

321 See Cobban: The Legacies of Collective Violence, [Subsection 7].

322 See Sarkin: The Tension Between Justice and Reconciliation in Rwanda, p. 152.

323 See Human Rights Watch: Uprooting the Rural Poor in Rwanda. Reconciliation, New York et al. 2001, in: http://www.hrw.org/reports/2001/rwanda/rwnvilg-12.htm#P1036_156804 (02.05.2008), [Paragraph 3].

324 See Walker: Rwandans Still Divided 10 Years On, [Subsections 5 and 6].

325 See Waugh: Paul Kagame and Rwanda, p. 155.

326 See International Crisis Group: Rwanda at the End of the Transition, pp. 16f.

327 See Nsengiyaremye: Zehn Jahre danach, p. 94.

328 See Reyntjens: Post-1994 Politics in Rwanda, p. 1113.

mainly Tutsi dominated.[329] Survivors, on the other hand, equally feel as the big losers of the RPF victory.[330]
Within the population it is meanwhile claimed that reconciliation between the peasants has worked; and that remaining problems lie with the ruling elite which has not yet embraced reconciliation.[331] This directly contradicts the government notion that an enlightened leadership is necessary to educate the people to resist political manipulation.[332] However, the RPF ignores the fact that most of the population does not view them as an enlightened leadership but rather as a foreign occupying force. People find it especially difficult to identify with president Kagame, as he grew up in Uganda and is anglophone as opposed to the great majority of francophone Rwandans. He is therefore viewed as a foreigner rather than a Rwandan.[333]
All in all, it is questionable if the RPF will succeed under these circumstances in creating a unified Rwandan identity and install their view on history as the leitmotif in Rwandan society.[334] Instead, it seems more likely that interethnic mistrust and animosities are fuelled by the RPF policies, be it military repression of large segments of the population or inequalities in housing.[335] There is a real danger that a vicious circle is manufactured by the RPF tactics in which the government uses repression to defend minority rule against a resentful Hutu majority and is viewed as an occupying force by Hutu. It might therefore create the very violent opposition it seeks to prevent.[336] The main goal of Rwanda's leadership today is creating a unified and single Rwandan identity. Yet, the way in which that goal is pursued is possibly dangerous for reconciliation. As Elizabeth Sidiropoulos points out: "The commitment of the current regime to ignore the spectre of ethnicity that continues to permeate much of society is both short-sighted and lacking in a truthful assessment of the costs in the future."[337] Separating ethnicity and power would be more feasible than suppressing ethnicity altogether. It has been the political instrumentalization of ethnicity that has facilitated violent outbursts in the past rather than personal attachment to ethnicity.[338] Today, ethnicity is abused by the government again. That amounts to grounds for serious concern, as minority rule over the

329 See Sarkin: The Tension Between Justice and Reconciliation in Rwanda, p. 153.
330 See International Crisis Group: Rwanda at the End of the Transition, p. 20.
331 See Longman/Rutagengwa: Memory, Identity and Community in Rwanda, p. 178.
332 See International Crisis Group: Rwanda at the End of the Transition, p. 5.
333 See Waugh: Paul Kagame and Rwanda, p. 221.
334 See Stroh: Legitimation allein durch Entwicklung?, p. 5.
335 See Wierzynska: Consolidating Democracy through Rwanda's Transitional Gacaca Courts, p. 1968.
336 See Sarkin: The Tension Between Justice and Reconciliation in Rwanda, p. 149.
337 Sidiropoulos: Democratisation and Militarisation in Rwanda, [Subsection 3.2, last paragraph].
338 See Drumbl: Punishment, Postgenocide, p. 1300.

majority population is closely linked to the occurrence of genocide. Marc Drumbl therefore fears: "So long as ethnicity is the driving force of Rwandan politics, the prospect of another genocide (...) looms on the horizon."[339] Unfortunately, precisely the horrific experience of genocide leads the Tutsi to cling to their monopoly of power. They need to understand that insisting on that monopoly as a precondition for their survival will not lead to reconciliation and peace. Rather, allowing for democracy and an equal sharing of power will make reconciliation and ending ethnic violence possible.[340] South Africa's example has shown that political leaders can enhance reconciliation and peace through dialogue. In Rwanda, the opposite seems to be the case.[341]

Banning ethnicity will not work. Ethnic hatred has been implanted in Rwandans for at least three decades. It will probably take as much time to overcome it.[342] Simultaneously, exclusion of one group from power in Rwanda has always been a disaster, as this group will inevitably try to take back power at a later stage.[343] If the RPF government continues to rely on colonial "divide and rule" tactics it will not overcome negative emotions and divisions in Rwandan society which hinder reconciliation at present.[344] As long as criticism cannot be voiced by suppressed groups in society and existing ethnic cleavages are not recognized in an attempt to rewrite history in a RPF sense, the current stability in Rwanda is likely to remain fragile. Peace and reconciliation could very well turn into violence and ethnic confrontation again.[345] So the question asked in the title of this chapter can be answered negatively. Repressive minority rule will not bridge the ethnic divide and provide the grounds for reconciliation, but rather intensify tensions and pose an obstacle to reconciliation and dealing with the past.

339 Drumbl: Punishment, Postgenocide, p. 1312.

340 See Mamdani: When Victims Become Killers, p. 279.

341 See Gobodo-Madikizela: Trauma und Versöhnung, p. 35.

342 See Walker: Genocide Hatred Lingers in Rwanda Schools, [Subsection 3].

343 See Lederach: Building Peace, p. 177.

344 See Sarkin: The Tension Between Justice and Reconciliation in Rwanda, p. 154.

345 See Hofmeier: Soziokulturelle Kurzanalyse Ruanda, p. 19.

5 Legal answers to the genocide: Justice and reconciliation in Rwanda

5.1 Transitional Justice

Transitional justice as a paradigm has gained momentum only fairly recently and touches diverse scientific fields like political science, sociology and law. It is concerned with societies that have been characterized by extreme violence in the past and are in the process of a political transformation[346] after a regime change.[347] Transitional justice studies examine how post-conflict societies deal with past atrocities, usually committed by the previous regime.[348] It thus refers to the relation of law and justice to political change in the context of political transformation. Debates in this field generally are divided in idealist and realist notions of the concept. In a realist view political change has to precede legal answers, which in turn are framed by the political system evolving. The other side holds that legal steps are necessary as a basis for political transition. In Rwanda legal answers to the genocide are clearly framed by the newly involved system as will be shown in this chapter.[349] Whatever school of thought one follows, the decision which path to pursue in transitional justice and whether a truth commission, trials or amnesty are the appropriate option, is crucial for future peace.[350] Aneta Wierzynska argues that the focus point has to be democratization rather than justice if transitional justice aims at altering the conditions that led to violence within a society.[351] However, transitional justice is framed by certain real-life circumstances that can amount to serious constraints, namely: the interests of those in power, security, available (legal)

346 For a definition of the term "transformation" see: Wichard Woyke (ed.): Handwörterbuch Internationale Politik, 8th updated edition, Bonn 2000 (Schriftenreihe Bundeszentrale für politische Bildung Band 404), p. 398. In Anglo-Saxon literature the term "transition" is mainly used to describe the transformation of (usually) a non-democratic to a democratic regime, which normally starts with multi-party elections and then sets in motion a transitional process in the political, social and judicial sphere, see Richard Sandbrook: Transitions Without Consolidation. Democratization in Six African Cases, in: Third World Quarterly, Vol. 17 (1996) 1, p. 85.

347 See Schilling: Gegen das Vergessen, p. 114f.

348 See David A. Crocker: Transitional Justice and International Civil Society, in: Alexsandar Jokie (ed.): War Crimes and Collective Wrongdoing, Oxford 2001, p. 270.

349 See Ruti G. Teitel: Transitional Justice, Oxford/New York 2000, p. 3.

350 See Betts: Should Approaches to Post-Conflict Justice and Reconciliation Be Determined Globally, Nationally or Locally?, p. 737.

351 See Wierzynska: Consolidating Democracy through Rwanda's Transitional Gacaca Courts, p. 1967.

resources in the country and the involvement of the international community.[352] The interests of the government have been laid out in chapter 4 and serve as a basis for the analysis of the legal responses to the genocide. The following chapter deals with transitional approaches in Rwanda and keeps the resource question, lack of security and the role of the international community in mind.

5.1.1 Retributive and restorative justice in transitional justice theory

Retributive justice views crimes as a violation of law and therefore they are regarded as an affair between the perpetrator and the state. The right for revenge does not belong to the violated party, i.e. the victim, but is mandated by the state.[353] Retribution then is not simple vengeance, but vengeance is framed by a third party that guarantees the respect of individual rights.[354] It can thus limit the individual desire for revenge by the victims, as they can see justice being done by an official body.[355] Luc Huyse identifies six advantages of retributive justice as a tool for reconciliation: Preventing private revenge and vigilante justice, preventing the perpetrators from gaining back power in a post-conflict situation, rehabilitating victims and acknowledging their suffering, individualizing guilt, strengthening democracy and ending impunity.[356] Gunnar Theissen adds that it can make the reintegration of innocent suspects easier, and that trials as the main form of retributive justice can send a clear message that murder and violations of law are criminal acts and cannot go unpunished. However, trials also have serious shortcomings: Resources might be lacking and proper representation of offenders not possible; they could provoke violent resistance from followers of the previous regime and victims might reject them as they don't trust the criminal system. Even though they are costly and time-consuming they often bring only selected individuals to trial as perpetrators might have fled or died. If offenders are set free due to lack of evidence and this fact is coupled with selective prosecution people might lose trust in criminal justice. A serious obstacle is the possibility of victor's justice and the perception of the population that the system is partisan. Furthermore, criminal justice is not victim-centred and therefore gives more

---

352 See Barsalou: Trauma and Transitional Justice in Divided Societies, p. 3.

353 See Brounéus: Reconciliation. Theory and Practice for Development Cooperation, p. 29.

354 See Minow: Between Vengeance and Forgiveness, p. 12.

355 See Betts: Should Approaches to Post-Conflict Justice and Reconciliation Be Determined Globally, Nationally or Locally?, p. 744.

356 See Luc Huyse: Justice, in: David Bloomfield/Teresa Barnes/Luc Huyse (eds.): Reconciliation After Violent Conflict. A Handbook, Stockholm 2003 (IDEA), in: http://www.idea.int/publications/reconciliation/upload/reconciliation_full.pdf (12.01.2008), p. 98.

attention to perpetrators than victims, which can be counterproductive to healing.[357] A point worth noticing in the context of reconciliation is the issue of truth. As trials aim at finding verdicts in terms of guilt they can restrict the flow of information and be counterproductive to establishing truth.[358]

Regardless of the advantages and risks of trials it is clear that retributive justice is a predominantly Western notion of criminal prosecution. Its focus on individual guilt runs counter to perceptions of justice in other cultures.[359] Nevertheless it has become the dominant paradigm in transitional justice, probably because the field is dominated by Western scholars. The focus on trials, however, often neglects other possible forms of dealing with the past.[360] It also fails to include forgiveness as a political concept into the legal process and seems oblivious to the effects of crimes on victims and their relatives. Other cultures are much more aware of the fact that there is more to justice than punishment.[361]

Restorative justice has been the dominant paradigm of justice all over the world for centuries and has been replaced by retributive justice dominated by central state power only fairly recently. In indigenous cultures these traditions have persisted until today.[362] Restorative justice, Desmond Tutu argues, is much closer to African culture than Western retributive justice. It follows the spirit of *ubuntu* and tries to mend broken relationships instead of punishing offenders. It aims at rehabilitation of both victim and perpetrator and reintegration.[363] The victim acquires a much more central role in restorative justice and is not excluded and ignored as in a retributive approach. Instead, the wishes and demands of victims are acknowledged and their view on appropriate punishment taken into account. The attitude towards offenders also differs considerably from a strictly punitive approach. Restorative justice acknowledges that the perpetrator is still part of the community and cannot simply be cut out and segregated from society through imprisonment. Instead, repentance and admission of guilt can make reintegration of offenders possible.[364]

Therefore restorative justice is making way for a shared future, by including forgiveness in the judicial process and concentrating on the healing of the vic-

357 See Theißen: Supporting Justice, Coexistence and Reconciliation After Armed Conflict, p. 3.

358 See Huyse: Justice, p. 104.

359 See Schilling: Gegen das Vergessen, p. 144.

360 See Fletcher/Weinstein: Violence and Social Repair, pp. 582f.

361 See Shriver: Where and When in Political Life Is Justice Served by Forgiveness?, p. 35.

362 See John Braithwaite: Restorative Justice and Responsive Regulation, Oxford/New York 2002, p. 5.

363 See Tutu: No Future Without Forgiveness, p. 51.

364 See Gerry Johnstone: Restorative Justice. Ideas, Values, Debates, Portland 2005, pp. 12f.

tim, whereas retributive justice is backward looking in its dealing with the past.[365] The involved parties in the justice process in a restorative concept do not simply include the perpetrator and the state, but rather the perpetrator, the victim and society. It focuses on the individual in a given conflict.[366] The inclusion of society is crucial if justice aims at repairing relationships in a community. As has been explained in chapter 2, restoration of relationships is an integral part of reconciliation. Thus it can be argued that restorative justice is a good instrument to achieve reconciliation, even though reconciliation is not the unavoidable outcome of such a process as various conditions influence it.[367]

However, restorative justice is very demanding for victims, as asking forgiveness is such an integral part of the concept. A highly traumatized survivor of atrocities might not be ready to restore relationships with the harm-doer who inflicted the suffering on him.[368] Furthermore, the reparation that is usually included in a restorative approach is not possible in cases of murder when the loss of a human life cannot be compensated.[369]

Despite these shortcomings, Marc Drumbl argues that dealing with the past and preventing future violence in Rwanda requires a restorative rather than retributive approach. As society in Rwanda is highly interdependent and so many people participated in the genocide, public shaming through restorative approaches is much more effective than placing guilt on individuals through trials.[370] Luc Huyse agrees and states that in the light of retributive shortcomings and the questionable alternative of amnesty, restorative justice opens a new way of dealing with the past in complex post-conflict societies like Rwanda.[371]

5.1.2 The importance of justice in Rwanda: Ending the culture of impunity

There are two main concepts at the disposal of a new leadership in the aftermath of violent conflict. One option is justice that can function as a collective cleansing process and rehabilitates the victims. The other is amnesty and a closure of history books which is said to lead to reconciliation by some researchers. However, this is challenged by many scholars who argue that rec-

---

365 See Forsberg: The Philosophy and Practice of Dealing with the Past, p. 71.

366 See Brounéus: Reconciliation. Theory and Practice for Development Cooperation, p. 29.

367 See Amstutz: Is Reconciliation Possible After Genocide?, pp. 554f.

368 See Lehmann: Thesenpapier, p. 7.

369 See Schilling: Gegen das Vergessen, p. 155.

370 See Drumbl: Punishment, Postgenocide, p. 1323.

371 See Huyse: Justice, p. 114.

onciliation cannot work if past atrocities are not dealt with.[372] In Rwanda, amnesty had never been an option, even though it might seem to be the easiest path to follow given the enormous number of genocide suspects. But the government ruled amnesty out from the start and pointed out that the culture of impunity did not allow for murderers to go free once again. It is indeed a special characteristic of Rwanda that it had been normal to kill Tutsi for decades without being punished. So ending the culture of impunity can be regarded as a basis for reconciliation.[373]

Not only the government, but also ordinary Rwandans demanded justice after the genocide and regarded it as a prerequisite for peaceful coexistence.[374] For Rwandans, issues like peace, reconciliation, justice and mercy are interdependent and therefore there can be no peace without justice.[375] Justice can even go so far that some Rwandan people demanded the death penalty for killers or even their families in surveys conducted in 1995. This clearly shows the importance of retribution for Rwandans.[376] Alison Des Forges underlines that point and claims that without the relief which justice can bring to a traumatized society, reconciliation will not be possible. According to her, justice in Rwanda is necessary for two reasons: First, the culture of impunity can be brought to an end, and second, prosecuting *genocidaires* can lay a foundation for future rule of law and is therefore an important tool in the transition to democracy.[377]

While all scholars agree that justice must end the culture of impunity and the past must be actively dealt with for future peace, the how is much more disputed. As clear as it seems that the horrific events in 1994 need to be addressed: if one assumes that it was normal for Hutu to kill Tutsi and that they responded obediently to their rulers who told them that it was not a crime to murder Tutsi, then how, in Marc Drumbls words, can one punish normalcy?[378] How, as Helena Cobban asks, can "normal" justice apply to Hutu who acted in abnormal circumstances?[379] Mamdani states that the RPF found itself at a historical crossroads after they took power and ended the genocide. The new rulers had two options: they could continue the civil war with the remaining elements of the old regime, or they could opt for political reconciliation that is not framed in terms of victory and defeat. Similarly, two kinds

372 See Huyse: The Process of Reconciliation, pp. 26 and 30.
373 See Schilling: Gegen das Vergessen, pp. 217f.
374 See Fisiy: Of Journeys and Border Crossings, pp. 22f.
375 See Burns/McGrew/Todorovic: Imagine Coexistence Pilot Projects in Rwanda and Bosnia, p. 90.
376 See Vandeginste: Rwanda, p. 270.
377 See Des Forges: Leave None to Tell the Story, p. 747.
378 See Drumbl: Punishment, Postgenocide, p. 1252.
379 See Cobban: The Legacies of Collective Violence, [Subsection 8].

of justice stood at their disposal: victor's justice, linked to continued civil war, and survivor's justice as a part of reconciliation.[380] The next chapter will lay out how the government pursued victor's justice in the beginning and later acknowledged the need for reconciliation.

5.1.3 A change in strategy: From conventional retributive to traditional restorative justice

From the outset the RPF pursued a retributive, vengeful approach of justice. Retribution as a prevention for further violence was the dominant paradigm and reconciliation was not publicly used in political discourse during the first five years after the genocide. When confronted with the suggestion of the establishment of a truth commission by South African delegates, the RPF dismissed it as irrelevant. There was no need for truth, they argued, as everyone knew what they had done. Instead, perpetrators must be punished.[381] In Kagame's view justice and retribution through proper trials of the guilty had to precede forgiveness and would then contribute to reconciliation automatically.[382]

Contrary to most observers Mamdani claims that the government early acknowledged the need for justice in a wider sense and realized that pure retribution would not be enough. But it was difficult to extend that notion to society, as people demanded justice to be done. So the RPF stuck with victor's justice in the beginning.[383] But the prosecution of a large segment of society led an inadequate system to face an overflow in detainees which it could not handle. Compromises had to be made. Furthermore, the extensive imprisonment criminalized Rwandan politics without contributing to institutional reform.[384] It was estimated that it would take 200 years to bring all genocide suspects before a court, and by 2002 it was obvious that the challenge of justice after the genocide was more than the government could handle[385] and that local forms of justice would be needed to deal with the genocide.[386] Research-

380 See Mamdani: When Victims Become Killers, p. 270.

381 See Schilling: Gegen das Vergessen, pp. 217 and 219.

382 See Prunier: The Rwanda Crisis, p. 343.

383 See Mamdani: From Conquest to Consent, p. 20.

384 See Drumbl: Punishment, Postgenocide, pp. 1286f.

385 See Kusi Hornberger: Rwandan Gacaca Courts in Crisis. Is There a Case for Judicial Review?, in: Africa Policy Journal, Vol. 3 (2007), in: http://www.hks.harvard.edu/kssgorg/apj/issues/spring_2007_issue/pdfs/Kusi.article.pdf (12.03.2008), pp. 4f. Others estimate the duration of trials to be a century. But numbers do not matter as the time spans include several generations in any case and are therefore unacceptable.

386 See Brounéus: Reconciliation. Theory and Practice for Development Cooperation, p. 10.

ers at "Penal Reform International" argue that the shift in government strategy came even earlier and that the RPF began to seek alternatives to the conventional system in 1998, which later led to the adoption of the Gacaca law in 2001.[387] The latter view is probably the most liable, but the year 2002 marks the beginning of the Gacaca pilot phase and therefore serves as a crossroads too. Wherever one fixes the turning point, the government undertook a noticeable shift in strategy when it turned from retributive trials to traditional Gacaca sessions. Even though the shift might have had ideological reasons as well, it can be regarded as a fact that the overcrowded prisons were highly costly for an economy in shambles and that valuable manpower for Rwanda's agriculture was lacking as most of the male workforce remained behind bars. These factors certainly contributed to the government's decision to abandon a purely vengeful path that aims at punishment instead of reintegration.[388]

5.2 Retributive justice in Rwanda

5.2.1 The International Criminal Tribunal for Rwanda (ICTR) – Can international justice contribute to reconciliation in Rwanda?

As a response to the Rwandan genocide the UN Security Council adopted a resolution to establish an international tribunal for the prosecution of the genocide in November 1994, which should be held in Arusha, Tanzania.[389] The establishment of the "International Criminal Tribunal for Rwanda" (ICTR) is widely regarded as a means to ease the guilt of the international community – which had failed to stop the genocide despite the presence of an UN peacekeeping force – that pays little attention to the needs of Rwandan society in dealing with the past.[390] The international community created a retributive response to genocidal atrocities which it deemed appropriate to end the culture of impunity, without consulting the Rwandan people.[391] Paul Gready argues that the ICTR simply serves the interests of the international community without paying attention to the survivors. It is therefore "an example of international justice by and for the international community"[392]. Reconciliation in Rwanda is not the main goal of the ICTR, which is more concerned with justice outside of Rwanda and the court's contribution to international law, especially with regard to the "International Criminal Court"

387 See Penal Reform International: Integrated Report on Gacaca Research and Monitoring, p. 6.
388 See Graybill: Pardon, Punishment, and Amnesia, p. 1122.
389 See UN Security Council: Security Council Resolution 955 on 8th November 1994.
390 See for example Waugh: Paul Kagame and Rwanda, p. 169.
391 See Tiemessen: After Arusha, p. 60.
392 Gready: Reconceptualising Transitional Justice, pp. 9 and 11.

(ICC).[393] It is in this area that the biggest successes of the ICTR can be found. In international legal terms, the ICTR is groundbreaking. It managed to achieve the first conviction for the crime of genocide by an international court in history, and the interim prime minister of Rwanda in 1994, Jean Kambanda, was the first person to plead guilty on charges of genocide. Moreover, rape was instituted as a crime against humanity and convictions in that area were achieved.[394] Additionally, if the desire for vengeance felt by the Rwandan people can be eased when they see the ringleaders of the genocide be punished, the ICTR also can contribute positively to justice in Rwanda.[395] It can therefore be regarded as a success that some of the masterminds of the genocide are now in custody in Arusha.[396] But apart from these rare positive points, the achievements of the ICTR have been rather slim, especially when the relevance of the court for reconciliation inside Rwanda is analyzed. The downside of the Arusha proceedings will be laid out in this chapter.

First, the focus on individuals, as much as it might be important for Rwandans to see them behind bars, is rather ill-suited to address the underlying causes of the genocide. The Rwandan leaders incited the killings in 1994; the hatred between the two antagonistic groups, however, had existed and grown for decades. The organizers of the genocide simply had to pull some strings to make the mixture of deep-rooted fears, ethnic hatred and divisive myths explode. If peace for Rwanda is to be achieved, the causal factors of the violence have to be addressed. Focusing on individuals as the main objects in dealing with the genocide neglects the fact that neighbours turned against neighbours without much hesitation. Without dispersing the deep-rooted hatred, prosecuting the leaders will not stop ethnic violence.[397]

Second, the court is far removed from the Rwandan population. Even though Arusha is geographically close to Rwanda's borders, it is hard to reach for ordinary citizens that cannot afford a plane ticket. So the Rwandan public is widely excluded from the proceedings in Tanzania. Furthermore, the legal procedures of international retributive justice are alien to Rwandans. They are used to bringing up complaints in person to local authorities. Now they have to access justice via distant procedural bodies that do not speak their language and are difficult to meet in person without appointments and lengthy procedures. These circumstances lead to the perception of victims that they are not well represented and that their suffering is not acknowledged by the court. Additionally, the long duration of the cases and the complicated presentation

393 See Betts: Should Approaches to Post-Conflict Justice and Reconciliation Be Determined Globally, Nationally or Locally?, p. 741.

394 See Uvin/Mironko: Western and Local Approaches to Justice in Rwanda, p. 220.

395 See Prunier: The Rwanda Crisis, p. 342.

396 See Des Forges: Leave None to Tell the Story, p. 744.

397 See Maogoto: The International Criminal Tribunal for Rwanda, pp. 70 and 73.

of evidence with respect to the rights of the accused are hardly understandable for people that are used to seeing matters dealt with within a few days.[398] As a result of these circumstances, the ICTR is widely unknown in Rwanda. Even though people know it exists, they have generally no idea what is going on in Arusha and what the court's work has to do with them.[399] An information centre in Kigali has been established to improve knowledge of the population but has done little to promote the court's work in Rwanda.[400]

Even if Rwandans are aware of the events in Tanzania, the court's performance does hardly help to improve its image in Rwanda. Courtroom management is disastrous and contributes to lengthy proceedings that often produce chaotic hearings. Working habits are another source of concern, as not all employees seem to be as dedicated to their work as they should be.[401] Apart from mismanagement, inefficiency, political tensions, slowness and corruption add to the negative image of the ICTR.[402] The attorneys are paid very favourably and receive extra money for business class travels. Some defence attorneys have split their salary with their clients and gave jobs to relatives and friends. Two defence investigators have even been excluded as credible allegations of their own involvement in the genocide surfaced. That does of course not contribute to Rwandans confidence in the court, even more so as the court had 256.9 million US Dollar (USD) to its expense in 2003 while "Official Development Assistance" (ODA) for Rwanda's roughly 8 million people amounted to only 322 million USD in 2000.[403] The budget of the court is twice the amount the Rwandan court system has received from the international community. Yet, despite the huge funding the slowness of the court (which managed to hear only 30 cases in five years) is creating bitter ill will in Rwanda and elsewhere.[404]

The fourth major problem with the ICTR lies in the fact that neither group in Rwanda is interested in the ICTR. The Hutu extremists feel they are being prosecuted as a consequence of their loss of power and fail to acknowledge their guilt. Therefore the court fails in its didactic approach. The Tutsi leadership wants to see the guilty punished, which in the first years after the genocide meant the death penalty, and feel the ICTR verdicts are much too light for the severity of the crimes. Until extremists on both sides arrive at judging

---

398 See Des Forges: Leave None to Tell the Story, p. 746.

399 See Uvin/Mironko: Western and Local Approaches to Justice in Rwanda, p. 221.

400 See Wegemund: Nationale Aussöhnung in Ruanda, p. 367.

401 See Cobban: Healing Rwanda, [Subsection 3].

402 See Gready: Reconceptualising Transitional Justice, p. 11.

403 See Cobban: Healing Rwanda, [Subsection 3].

404 See Theißen: Supporting Justice, Coexistence and Reconciliation After Armed Conflict, p. 4.

the violence as wrong (and vengeance, in the case of the Tutsi) the court will have little impact on attitudes in Rwanda and fail to deter future violence.[405]
Another closely connected factor is the perception of Hutu that the trials only shed light on the genocide while the violence against Hutu is ignored. As RPF crimes are not prosecuted in Arusha, the court creates one-dimensional justice and a Manichean distinction between the good Tutsi victims and the bad Hutu *genocidaires*.[406] Some even call the tribunal ironically TPIH (from the French acronym TPIR): "le Tribunal Penal International pour les Hutu".[407] So while the Tutsi regard the ICTR as a waste of money and feel it should be held in Rwanda, the Hutu demand the prosecution of RPF crimes as a condition for their acceptance of the court.[408] But as long as the RPF controls the court and fails to cooperate with it the perception of victor's justice will remain and Hutu will not accept the truth established by the ICTR. This fact certainly is highly counterproductive to reconciliation.[409]
Some recent developments shortly before the mandate of the ICTR ends this year bear some hope that the role of the court will be perceived more positively in the future. Firstly, cases that cannot be tried before the deadline of the court will be transferred to Rwanda.[410] This has become possible through the abolition of the death penalty in Rwanda, which had been the major obstacle for trials to be held there.[411] Secondly, ICTR detainees can now serve their sentence in Rwanda, which had been a longstanding demand of the Rwandan government, and can therefore be regarded as an important breakthrough in the relations between the court and Rwanda.[412] However, a recent case has made the Rwandan government doubt that the ICTR is sincere in its cooperation with Rwanda as it has refused to transfer the accused leader of the Interahamwe militia[413], Yussuf Munyakazi, to Rwanda, saying he would not receive a fair trial in his home country.[414]

---

405 See Maogoto: The International Criminal Tribunal for Rwanda, pp. 77ff.
406 See Uvin/Mironko: Western and Local Approaches to Justice in Rwanda, p. 222.
407 See Zorbas: Reconciliation in Post-genocide Rwanda, p. 34.
408 See Longman/Pham/Weinstein: Connecting Justice to Human Experience, p. 215.
409 See Cobban: Healing Rwanda, [Subsection 5].
410 See Human Rights Watch: World Report 2008, p. 146.
411 See European Commission: European Commission Welcomes Abolition of the Death Penalty in Rwanda (26.07.2007), in: http://europa.eu/rapid/pressReleasesAction.do?reference=IP/07/1183&format=HTML&aged=1&language=EN&guiLanguage=en (16.03.2008).
412 See Robert Walker: Rwandan Jail for Genocide Guilty (04.03.2008), in: BBC News, in: http://news.bbc.co.uk/go/pr/fr/-/2/hi/africa/7277995.stm (10.3.2008), [Subsection 2].
413 The Interahamwe militia was composed of young men and one of the militias created by Hutu hardliners to carry out the genocide. They were attached to the ruling

In conclusion it can be said that the ICTR is groundbreaking in its contribution to international law but fails to contribute to reconciliation in Rwanda. Although this thesis does not provide a detailed account of the ICTR, it has been found that the overwhelming majority of scholars agree on this judgement.[415]

5.2.2 The national court system and its contribution to reconciliation

After the genocide, Rwandan state structures lay in ashes. The justice system was virtually not existent, staff had been killed, financial resources were lacking and court rooms had been destroyed. While the prisons suffered from serious overcrowding, the first court sessions were only held in late 1996.[416] With the help of the international community Rwanda managed to rebuild its legal system slowly. But soon after the judiciary had begun its work influential people from all walks of life and the military interfered with its proceedings.[417] Judges were not free from outside pressures and often incompetent and corrupt. The quality of justice has improved since 1998 but is still regarded as problematic. Furthermore, justice is highly politicized, a seemingly unavoidable outcome of post-genocide justice. The population on the other hand feels alienated by the formal justice system which is remote and foreign to them. Most people were too occupied with their daily struggle for survival to actively take part in the judicial process.[418]

The importance justice carried for the population became evident in April 1998, however. The government ordered public executions of 22 people found guilty on genocide charges (in trials that left serious doubts about their fairness), which were watched by tens of thousands in apparent excitement and bloodlust. The executions were meant to send a clear message to Rwandans that the cycle of impunity had come to an end and the rule of law would be established from now on in Rwanda. However, they led Martha Minow to

---

MRND party and were responsible for the most brutal killings of Tutsi; see Dallaire: Shake Hands With the Devil, pp. 129 and 462.

414 See Robert Walker: Rwanda Anger at Genocide Tribunal (30.05.2008), in: BBC News, in: http://news.bbc.co.uk/2/hi/africa/7427249.stm (01.06.2008), [Subsection 1].

415 See for example Oomen: Donor-Driven Justice, p. 896; Gready: Reconceptualising Transitional Justice, pp. 8f.

416 See Daja Wenke: Gacaca Rechtssprechung in Ruanda. Ein traditionelles Gerichtsverfahren in modernisierter Form. Struktur, Probleme und Chancen, in: Stichproben. Wiener Zeitschrift für kritische Afrikastudien, Vol. 2 (2002) 4, p. 26.

417 See Des Forges: Leave None to Tell the Story, p. 749.

418 See Uvin/Mironko: Western and Local Approaches to Justice in Rwanda, p. 225.

conclude: "Rather than ending the cycles of revenge, the trials themselves were revenge."[419]

The perception that justice in Rwanda is revenge, or victor's justice, is certainly the most worrying fact about the Rwandan attempt to bring genocide suspects to court. The justice system is dominated by Tutsi and experienced Hutu judges and prosecutors have been cut out of the process, depriving the already strained system of valuable personnel and enforcing the feelings of exclusion from the new Rwandan state by Hutu.[420] While virtually all suspects are Hutu, their judges are Tutsi, which is bound to trigger the deep-rooted inferiority complex of Hutu. Because Tutsi judicial staff work under a Tutsi dominated government that is far from democratic, their work follows the lines of the official truths that have been laid out in the previous chapters.[421] The perception of Hutu that victor's justice is practised in Rwanda is hard to dismiss. And as the victors are Tutsi and the losers are Hutu the same old ethnic antagonisms are replayed with the Tutsi rubbing their victory in the face of Hutu with every trial that takes place. Certainly these circumstances are highly problematic for reconciliation if one bears in mind the crucial role justice plays for reconciliation.[422] Justice, as much as it can contribute to reconciliation, will achieve the opposite if the government continues to assume that all Hutu alive are collectively responsible for the genocide.[423] Officially the government claims that lifting that burden is one of the main goals of the national trials but the way in which justice is carried out makes that claim doubtful. The fact that no RPF atrocities are tried before the national courts intensifies the perception that justice is biased in favour of the Tutsi.[424]

The above mentioned quality of justice is another source of concern. As the system is unable to detect false accusations people have repeatedly made false claims motivated by greed or political rivalries, and corruption remains high. False accusations have led to a growing number of innocent people in prison while known perpetrators remain at large, sometimes due to bribery. Trials progress very slowly, an unacceptable fact regarding the swelling prison population and inhumane detention conditions. Estimations have been made that it would take hundreds of years to try all suspects if the pace is not accelerated. Judicial staff is poorly paid and works under a lot of pressure from all sides, which might explain their inefficiency. Judges received minimal training and are mostly inexperienced as most of the experienced judicial staff has been

---

419 Minow: Between Vengeance and Forgiveness, p. 124.

420 See Sarkin: The Tension Between Justice and Reconciliation in Rwanda, p. 158.

421 See Lemarchand: Genocide in the Great Lakes, p. 13.

422 See Maogoto: The International Criminal Tribunal for Rwanda, p. 85.

423 See Strizek: Zur Lage der Menschenrechte in Ruanda, p. 39.

424 See Betts: Should Approaches to Post-Conflict Justice and Reconciliation Be Determined Globally, Nationally or Locally?, p. 746

killed in the genocide. Defendants have often no counsel, a clear sign that due process is lacking. Witnesses are often harassed by relatives of the accused and feel at risk if they stand up in court, as do the members of the judiciary in general.[425] Judges face an impossible task. Tutsi judges will always be suspected to act in the government's will, while the few Hutu judges can attract the anger of their own group when being too harsh and are labelled sympathizers of *genocidaires* if they are too soft. For neither group is it possible to avoid the image of being partisan.[426] The lacking quality of justice deepens the perception of Rwandans that the formal court system is neither fair nor of any relevance to them. Instead it is regarded as alien and remote.[427] The question then is: How can a remote and alien procedure that is furthermore seen as unjust and biased contribute to reconciliation?

The Rwandan legal system has seen some remarkable improvements over the years. While more and more people have been acquitted less people have received life imprisonment or death penalties. But given the extraordinary situation the system faces this has not been enough.[428] The still slow pace and the high detainee population carry a high frustration potential for both victims and the accused. The swift justice that would be needed is impossible to deliver in face of the limited capacities in Rwanda. Some have claimed that the RPF is keeping the prisoner population high on purpose to remind the world of its failure in the Rwandan crisis and improve security inside the country.[429] If that was really the case, the strategy could be judged as extremely shortsighted and lacking a thorough assessment of the situation given the extreme burden the situation in jails and communal lock-ups places on the reconciliation process.

To conclude: There have been improvements in the national management of genocide trials and Rwanda still manages to judge a considerably higher number of suspects than the ICTR. Due process is lacking but perhaps understandably under the circumstances. No justice system in the world, not even in developed countries, could handle such a high number of suspects in an acceptable time span. The problem lies in the politicized nature of the justice delivered. Most Rwandans do not view the state and judiciary as serving the interests of all citizens, but of the victorious RPF. The verdicts are regarded as the products of biased victor's justice and impunity is not ended but rather perpetuated as RPF crimes in the civil war and human rights violations of the

---

425 See Des Forges: Leave None to Tell the Story, pp. 754ff. Des Forges has documented cases of harassment, bribery and corruption in this extensive study for Human Rights Watch.

426 See Waugh: Paul Kagame and Rwanda, p. 177.

427 See Gready: Reconceptualising Transitional Justice, p. 12.

428 See Uvin/Mironko: Western and Local Approaches to Justice in Rwanda, p. 223.

429 See Waugh: Paul Kagame and Rwanda, pp. 175f.

RPA are not brought before the courts. Victims, themselves important actors in the reconciliation process, often do not know that hearings in courts are taking place and are therefore robbed of their chance to receive compensation.[430] Biased, politicized justice and overcrowded prisons are certainly not creating the circumstances for reconciliation and justice as an essential part of it. This chapter therefore concludes that the national court system in Rwanda is, in its present form, not contributing to reconciliation. However, it has achieved much more for justice than the ICTR.

5.2.3 Assessment of the impact of formal retributive justice to reconciliation in Rwanda

Neither the ICTR nor the formal domestic court system in Rwanda, both modelled after a Western understanding of justice, have been able to fulfil the needs of Rwanda in the quest for justice. The slowness, remoteness (both geographically and socially), enormous costs, corruption and political pressure have contributed to the fact that only little justice has been achieved for Rwandans.[431] The same holds true for the issue of truth. While courts establish truth beyond doubt in lengthy procedures that might even lead to the acquittal of suspects for the lack of evidence, this kind of truth is not the truth needed in post-genocidal societies. Instead, it might even foster conflict between adversary ethnic groups that cling to their collective myths. Victims in particular might find the truth established by formal justice unsatisfactory, as they gain little knowledge about the fate of their relatives. For them, the ICTR and the national courts have achieved neither justice nor truth, both essential parts of reconciliation.[432] Problematic with regard to truth is also the fact that courts always create one official truth and produce winners or losers of a case. In a society where either side feels victimised the division into winners and losers will simply strengthen the perception of victor's justice and not help to unite the two sides of the ethnic divide. To the contrary, it might create new conflicts.[433] Additionally, Western-style courts aim at establishing the facts about what happened, but the facts are not what victims are looking for. Signs of remorse are much more important for victims and can enhance their readiness to forgive and reconcile with the perpetrators. Formal court systems, however, do not include remorse in their proceedings and are therefore rather inhibiting reconciliation.[434]

---

430 See Vandeginste: Rwanda, pp. 266ff.

431 See Uvin/Mironko: Western and Local Approaches to Justice in Rwanda, pp. 19 and 29.

432 See Drumbl: Punishment, Postgenocide, pp. 1283 and 1289.

433 See Schilling: Gegen das Vergessen, pp. 139f.

434 See Cobban: Healing Rwanda, [Subsection 6].

Conventional justice might also be ill-suited as a response to mass violence as it concentrates on establishing individual guilt and fails to address group violence and collective responsibility.[435] It also fails to address the social conditions - like an authoritarian regime and underlying tensions between societal groups - that could plunge Rwanda back into violence.[436] The vicious circle of violence is not visible in Rwanda today but continues to boil under the surface. The ICTR and the national trials have not been able to end it but just send it underground. So far, the ICTR in particular has not contributed to peace, truth, respect for human rights and reconciliation in Rwanda by trying some of the big fish.[437] The failure to end the cycles of violence is inherent in criminal trials. Designed for "ordinary" criminals and "ordinary" crimes, their power to deter future violations of law fails in cases of mass violence, or *radical evil.* Deterrence works on the assumption of rational choice. In irrational circumstances like a genocide the choice to participate in violence will most likely not be based on rational thoughts. Drawing on this thought criminal trials might be the wrong response to mass violence altogether.[438]
The failure of the retributive justice approaches – both international and national – to contribute to reconciliation, justice and truth inside Rwanda has become obvious. Donna Pankhurst claims that the "failure of a punitive process is likely to have a worse impact on perceptions of justice than not having one at all."[439] Following this argument Rwanda's future looks rather grim. This is why more attention has to be paid to traditional approaches that leave the path of western legal concepts which apparently cannot solve the complex problems of post-genocide Rwanda on the path towards reconciliation.[440]

---

435 See Fletcher/Weinstein: Violence and Social Repair, p. 604.

436 See Wierzynska: Consolidating Democracy through Rwanda's Transitional Gacaca Courts, p. 1947.

437 See Maogoto: The International Criminal Tribunal for Rwanda, p. 91.

438 See Drumbl: Punishment, Postgenocide, pp. 1253f.

439 Pankhurst: Issues of Justice and Reconciliation in Complex Political Emergencies, p. 252.

440 See Volker Boege: Traditional Approaches to Conflict Transformation. Potentials and Limits, in: David Bloomfield/Martina Fischer/Beatrix Schmelzle (eds.): Berghof Handbook for Conflict Transformation, Berlin 2004, in: http://www.berghof-handbook.net/uploads/download/boege_handbook.pdf (02.06.2008), p. 3.

5.3 The Gacaca jurisdictions: "African Justice for African Healing?"[441]

5.3.1 Turning to alternative methods: The Gacaca jurisdictions in Rwanda

"Gacaca" is the Kinyarwanda word for "grass", and has been traditionally used for a place in Rwandan communities where villagers gather on the lawn and discuss problems within their community that need a solution and require acts of justice.[442] It traces back to pre-colonial times but was also used during colonization and after independence to complement the formal system in cases of customary law.[443] No law regulated the Gacaca meetings and issues were solved on a purely local level. Usually Gacaca sessions were held once a week and everyone living on the hill could attend, which people did in great numbers. Whoever had an issue to bring forward could speak and every community member was allowed to reply. In long debates the issue would then be resolved. Most of the matters brought forward at Gacaca were civil in nature, ranging from property disputes to unpaid debts, but injuries of persons were also possible issues to be brought up at Gacaca. In general, the disputes occurred between families, relatives or neighbours and only very few cases concerned people from other communes. In a study conducted by Filip Reyntjens it was found that more than 80 percent of the cases were solved during the discussions at Gacaca.[444] The Gacaca was chaired by the community elders who stood above the quarrelling parties. The aim of traditional Gacaca was always reconciliation. Offenders had to acknowledge their guilt when the elders found them guilty, and could be punished. But punishment and admission of guilt had the aim to restore the relationships within the community and reconcile offenders and victims; punishment was not an end in itself. Offenders had to accept the judgement or would face exclusion from the community which worked as a strong incentive to acknowledge guilt, as an exclusion from social rituals and community life is unthinkable in Rwandan society.[445] Traditional Gacaca was a very important informal conflict solving vehicle that sought mediation between families to establish social peace in a

---

441 Waugh: Paul Kagame and Rwanda, p. 173.

442 See Hornberger: Rwandan Gacaca Courts in Crisis, p. 6.

443 See Wenke: Gacaca Rechtssprechung in Ruanda, pp. 28f.

444 See Reyntjens: Le Gacaca ou la Justice du Gazon au Rwanda, pp. 32ff.

445 See Esther Mujawayo/Souad Belhaddad: Auf der Suche nach Stéphanie. Ruanda zwischen Versöhnung und Verweigerung, Wuppertal 2007, pp. 51f.

participatory and egalitarian way. The majority of the Rwandan population had a positive attitude towards Gacaca.[446]

As it dawned on the Rwandan leadership that attempting to judge all accused of genocide in the formal court system was impossible and the death of so many detainees in Rwandan prisons costly in political and social terms, it turned to Gacaca as a Rwandan tradition of conflict resolution. The traditional Gacaca was transformed into a modernized Gacaca called the Gacaca jurisdictions or tribunals.[447] In 2001, the Rwandan parliament approved of a law designed to set up Gacaca jurisdictions on different administrative levels, namely cell, sector, district and province. They are made up of a "General Assembly", a "Seat" (19 elected judges) and a "Coordinating Committee". On the cell level, the "General Assembly" consists of all inhabitants above the age of thirteen, for the higher levels "honest persons"[448] are chosen to constitute the Assembly. The task of the Gacaca jurisdictions is to judge all crimes of genocide or crimes against humanity between the first of October 1990 and the 31st of December 1994.[449] The accused were divided into four categories. The

446 See Reyntjens: Le Gacaca ou la Justice du Gazon au Rwanda, p. 39.

447 See Peter Uvin: The Gacaca Tribunals in Rwanda, in: David Bloomfield/Teresa Barnes/Luc Huyse (eds.): Reconciliation After Violent Conflict. A Handbook, Stockholm 2003 (IDEA), in: http://www.idea.int/publications/reconciliation/upload/reconciliation_full.pdf (12.01.2008), p. 116. This thesis will use the terms Gacaca jurisdictions, tribunals, courts, experiment and simply Gacaca which are all common in literature on the topic. If I refer to the traditional Gacaca it will be indicated.

448 Honest persons are defined by several characteristics, like always telling the truth, not being a known perpetrator in the genocide, having good morals and behaviour or being free from the spirit of sectarianism. See Organic Law N° 40/2000 of 26/01/2001 Setting up "Gacaca Jurisdictions" and Organizing Prosecutions for Offences Constituting the Crime of Genocide or Crimes Against Humanity Committed between October 1, 1990 and December 31, 1994, Kigali 2001, p. 5.

449 See Organic Law N° 40/2000, pp. 3ff. This law has been revised in 2004 and 2006 and certain articles have been amended after experiences on the ground during the pilot phase required changes in the law. See Organic Law N° 28/2006 of 27/06/2006 Organic Law Modifying and Complementing Organic Law n° 16/2004 of 19/06/2004 Establishing the Organisation, Competence and Functioning of Gacaca Courts Charged With Prosecuting and Trying the Perpetrators of the Crime of Genocide and Other Crimes Against Humanity, Committed Between October 1, 1990 and December 31, 1994, Kigali 2006, pp 2ff.

Another reform of the Gacaca courts in March 2007 extended the mandate of the Gacaca which can now impose life imprisonment instead of the previous maximum of 30 years. A new categorization of the accused also allows for more people to be tried in front of Gacaca than before in order to speed up the trials, see Human Rights Watch: World Report 2008, p. 145.

Aditionally, in 2004 a new National Department of Gacaca Courts has replaced the former Department of Gacaca Courts which was situated in the Supreme Court.

first category contains planners and ringleaders of the genocide and especially those that had positions of authority during the genocide. It also includes people accused of sexual torture or rape. The second category is made up of people who murdered or participated in attacks of persons that led to death. If a perpetrator did not cause death but serious injuries with the intent to kill he is also included in category 2. Category 3 was created for people that participated in attacks without the intent to kill. As this category turned out to be difficult to manage in practice it was abolished in 2004 and people in this category were placed in the second group. The last group contains people that committed attacks against property which usually results in reparation penalties instead of imprisonment. Since the re-structuring in 2004 this category is basically the third.[450]

Four phases were designed in the implementation of Gacaca. First an awareness raising campaign increased the knowledge about Gacaca before the Gacaca judges to chair the sessions were elected. In the third phase reconciliation and confession procedures were addressed and then some of the prisoners were reintegrated into society through work programs.[451] When the Gacaca courts started working they first gathered all information about known victims and perpetrators and the crimes committed in the area. Like in the traditional form the cases would then be debated and the "General Assembly" could participate in the process by giving testimony. In the end the "Seat" would reach a verdict. Every defendant can appeal his case at the Gacaca of the next higher level. Cases that fall under category 1 cannot be dealt with at Gacaca but remain in the formal court system.[452]

There has been much debate on the topic of the Rwandan Gacaca courts and whether they can still be described as a traditional Rwandan mechanism for conflict resolution. It is certainly right that a fundamental difference lies in the state-enforced manner in which the Gacaca courts operate today. While traditional Gacaca has been a matter of the community without state involvement and coercion, people now have to attend and the proceedings are mandated and overseen by the state. State law provides the basis for Gacaca today whereas informal traditions without stated legal norms characterized tradi-

---

The new department is now autonomous in administration and finances; see: Penal Reform International: From Camp to Hill, p. 4.

450 See Penal Reform International: Integrated Report on Gacaca Research and Monitoring, p. 11.

451 See Hornberger: Rwandan Gacaca Courts in Crisis, p. 7.

452 See Uvin/Mironko: Western and Local Approaches to Justice in Rwanda, p. 226. A list of category 1 suspects can be obtained at Rwanda Government: Rwandan Government List of Genocide Suspects, in: http://www.gov.rw/government/category1.htm (12.06.2008).

tional Gacaca.[453] Violations of informal community rules were dealt with at Gacaca in the past, whereas today violations of state law are subject of the sessions. However, the Rwandan government readily admits that the new Gacaca is not the same as Gacaca in a traditional sense but rather a way to deal with the past based on traditional mechanisms.[454] The altered name of the courts is one indication for this. The next chapter will discuss in what ways the Gacaca courts still function as a traditional vehicle and what implications this has for reconciliation.

Another debate revolves around the retributive and restorative character of the Gacaca courts and is closely connected to the issue of tradition. While most scholars agree that the Gacaca jurisdictions are a mixture of restorative and retributive justice and basically function as a truth commission and a tribunal at the same time[455], a PRI report argues that Gacaca is a judicial process that seeks punishment for the perpetrator and is therefore retributive in essence.[456] Alana Tiemessen challenges that notion and argues that Gacaca is essentially restorative, as it includes healing, confessions, admission of guilt and reintegration in the process and is therefore very distinct from the strictly punitive character of the ICTR or the national courts.[457]

5.3.2 Gacaca jurisdictions and reconciliation: A promising approach?

In implementing the Gacaca jurisdictions the government pursued several goals: trials should be expedited and therefore the prison system would be relieved and the life threatening conditions inside the prisons eased. The participation of the entire community should reveal the full truth of what happened during the civil war and genocide. The punitive character of Gacaca on the other hand should sweep out the culture of impunity in Rwanda. Furthermore, Gacaca should foster reconciliation between Rwandans and enable them to repair the broken ties between them.[458] President Kagame identifies justice (as an end to impunity) and reconciliation as the main goals of Gacaca. The government sets high hopes in the ability of Gacaca to contribute to rec-

---

453 See Vandeginste: Rwanda, p. 275.

454 See Tiemessen: After Arusha, p. 61.

455 See for example Betts: Should Approaches to Post-Conflict Justice and Reconciliation Be Determined Globally, Nationally or Locally?, p. 747; Richters/Dekker/De Jonge: Reconciliation in the Aftermath of Violent Conflict in Rwanda, p. 209; Wierzynska: Consolidating Democracy through Rwanda's Transitional Gacaca Courts, p. 1957.

456 See Penal Reform International: Integrated Report on Gacaca Research and Monitoring, p. 53.

457 See Tiemessen: After Arusha, p. 58.

458 See Penal Reform International: Integrated Report on Gacaca Research and Monitoring, p. 10.

onciliation but also acknowledges the difficulties of the process.[459] As this thesis is interested in the contribution of judicial approaches to reconciliation, Gacaca seems to be a promising example that needs to be further examined. All of its main goals follow the basic ingredients of reconciliation as laid out in chapter 2: relationships, truth, justice and reintegration. It will be analyzed how the goals work out in practice and if they can be achieved through Gacaca.

How traditional is Gacaca?

Most scholars state that Gacaca is a distinctly Rwandan mechanism and carries the features of traditional African conflict resolution. This leads to a high degree of acceptance within the Rwandan population as opposed to the attitudes displayed towards the Western forms of justice.[460] A major study conducted in 2001 by the John Hopkins University together with Rwandan authorities found that the great majority of people were in favour of Gacaca jurisdictions and believed them to become a success.[461] These favourable attitudes are surely due to the perception of people that Gacaca is traditional, as mechanisms aiming at justice and reconciliation are presumably always more effective when they are drawn on the cultural context.[462] In African societies conflicts are settled through discussions that aim at consensus, which is why confrontational trials used in Western cultures are rarely used.[463] The design of Gacaca laid out in the previous chapter is therefore clearly in line with traditional African conflict resolution. Moreover, reconciliation is the most important goal of traditional approaches, and also of Gacaca.[464]

---

459 See BBC: BBC Interview with Paul Kagame, in: http://www.gov.rw/government/president/interviews/2001/gacaca.html (13.06.2008).

460 See for example Daly: Between Punitive and Reconstructive Justice, p. 378; Wenke: Gacaca Rechtssprechung in Ruanda, p. 47. Bah has established negotiations, mediation and palaver as traditional African solutions in conflict situations in a renowned UNESCO publication. See Thierno Bah: Les Mécanismes traditionnels de prévention et de résolution des conflits en Afrique noire, in: Federico Mayor/Edouard Matoko (eds.): Les fondements endogènes d'une culture de la paix en Afrique. Mécanismes traditionnels de prévention et de résolution des conflits, Paris 1999 (UNESCO Publication), in: http://www.unesco.org/cpp/publications/mecanismes/edbah.htm (12.06.2008), [Subsection II.1 and II.2].

461 See Gabisirege/Babalola: Perceptions About the Gacaca Law in Rwanda, p. 13.

462 See Betts: Should Approaches to Post-Conflict Justice and Reconciliation Be Determined Globally, Nationally or Locally?, p. 748.

463 See Sarkin: The Tension Between Justice and Reconciliation in Rwanda, p. 165.

464 See Boege: Traditional Approaches to Conflict Transformation, p. 7.

However, there are serious concerns about Gacaca as a traditional approach that cannot be dismissed easily. Critics argue that the Gacaca jurisdictions bear little resemblance to the traditional instrument and that the state imposed manner might restrict popular participation.[465] While Gacaca is still local and engages the population, it is now mandated by the state and not voluntary anymore. Instead of the restoration of social peace the guilty go back to prison. It is that punitive function of the new Gacaca that changes the mechanism profoundly and makes it an instrument serving the state rather than the communities. State pressure replaces social pressure.[466] Therefore it might be inappropriate to call the Gacaca jurisdictions traditional and expect them to carry all the benefits of traditional approaches for reconciliation. In addition to the concerns about state coercion the effects of the genocide also have to be kept in mind. Social relationships and community organization as well as the specific set of values attached to ancient Gacaca have been radically altered by the genocide. If the basic conditions for a functioning traditional Gacaca are not in place in modern society, a traditional approach might not be the right answer to Rwanda's modern problems.[467]

Reconciliation at a grass roots level: The role of communities

Rebuilding the ruptured communities in Rwanda needs the acknowledgement of the communities of what happened during the genocide and therefore it is crucial for communities to deal with the past. The genocide was a communal affair, and therefore requires a communal response.[468] Gacaca, in Erin Daly's words, is "a populist response to a populist genocide"[469] and consequently a good approach to achieve reconciliation, as it values the notion that rebuilding the country lies within the population. Active participation in the justice process will influence people's perception of justice and also make it more difficult for the state to intervene and impose justice as the huge number of Gacaca sessions all over the country are difficult to control. Furthermore, Gacaca can bring the communities together and facilitate exchange between former enemies. They can install a common experience of creating justice together as

465 See Leah Werchick: Prospects for Justice in Rwanda's Citizen Tribunals, in: Human Rights Brief, Vol. 8 (2002) 3, in: http://www.wcl.american.edu/hrbrief/08/3rwanda.cfm, [Subsection 8].

466 See Betts: Should Approaches to Post-Conflict Justice and Reconciliation Be Determined Globally, Nationally or Locally?, p. 743. The reintegration of prisoners through work programs mentioned before aims at reintegration instead of prison punishment and is therefore a step towards a more restorative Gacaca.

467 See Schilling: Gegen das Vergessen, p. 343.

468 See Fletcher/Weinstein: Violence and Social Repair, p. 612.

469 See Daly: Between Punitive and Reconstructive Justice, p. 381.

opposed to the divisive experiences people made during the genocide.[470] Working together can help to rebuild social ties within the community and allow for peaceful coexistence. Usually this implies community work like rebuilding infrastructure, but working together for justice might be an even greater benefit for the success of a reconciliation process.[471]

Reconciliation is only possible between local actors that carry the lion's share of the reconciliation process. The process is framed by the state or international efforts but in the end the ability to reconcile of ordinary people determine its success.[472] Therefore justice mechanisms also have to be embedded in communities and involve and engage local actors to achieve democracy and justice, and reconciliation in the long run, in a post-conflict state.[473] This is exactly what Gacaca is doing. Members of the community have to communicate with each other, which is the first step towards coexistence. The manner of dispute settlement can function as a steam valve on a communal level. Letting people make their suffering public in the community can be beneficial for reconciliation.[474]

Certainly there are risks attached to community justice as well. First, the possibility of renewed confrontations in the community through Gacaca is very real. Bringing up the events again in the community could generate hatred and mistrust instead of reconciliation.[475] Second, if the state tries to control Gacaca this could seriously limit the acceptance of the local population, and the contribution to reconciliation. People need to regard Gacaca as their own rather than a state-imposed justice vehicle, as top-down approaches will not work in the local communities due to the extreme fear and suspicion of the population.[476] These risks are real. But if it is true that the government cannot possibly control all the Gacaca sessions, the communal element of Gacaca can foster reconciliation and the rebuilding of social ties, even though occasional ruptures might occur at times.

Airing the truth through Gacaca

Chapter 2 established the importance of truth for reconciliation. The emphasis should, however, be placed on dialogical truth that is retrieved through

470 See Daly: Between Punitive and Reconstructive Justice, pp. 376f.

471 See Spelman: Coexistence and Repair, p. 249.

472 See Theißen: Supporting Justice, Coexistence and Reconciliation After Armed Conflict, p. 13.

473 See Gready: Reconceptualising Transitional Justice, pp. 9f.

474 See Wierzynska: Consolidating Democracy through Rwanda's Transitional Gacaca Courts, pp. 1954ff.

475 See Uvin/Mironko: Western and Local Approaches to Justice in Rwanda, p. 227.

476 See Vandeginste: Rwanda, pp. 275ff.

personal exchange of people. The structure of Gacaca can bring about that dialogical truth and function as a quasi truth and reconciliation commission.[477] Gacaca is an inexpensive mechanism to hear all the facts and piece together truth about what has happened.[478] Bringing together different accounts of the past at Gacaca can create a full picture and maybe also a shared account of the past that replaces the different versions of history existing among the different groups.[479] Truth is extremely important for survivors. As perpetrators are forced to speak at Gacaca it is brought to light and the silence that haunts the survivors is broken.[480] As only perpetrators carry the necessary information about what happened to the survivors' families it is crucial to make them speak.[481] The healing process of the victims can only start when the truth about what happened is aired.[482]

Bringing the truth to light is not easy at Gacaca, however. Perpetrators, bystanders and even survivors refuse to reveal the truth and potential witnesses are often intimidated. As a consequence, people do not testify out of fear and the lack of witnesses damages Gacaca severely.[483] Witnesses have been killed and silenced and their security cannot be guaranteed by the authorities. It is understandable that many rather keep silent under such circumstances. Survivors are among the group that speaks out the most, which shows the divide between them and the silent mass of Hutu.[484] It has been noticed that especially Hutu and non-survivors show very little interest and tend to abstain from participating. This fact is clearly an obstacle to finding the truth if the quest for facts relies upon the participation of people. Released prisoners often testify to only some crimes or accuse others so that half-truths, omissions, outright lies and false testimony are common.[485] People blame crimes on dead or exiled persons in order to spare their comrades, or even settle private scores by blaming persons they have a conflict with.[486] Many defendants feel they have been accused because someone wants to have their property and get them out of the way. As accused are mainly Hutu and the beneficiaries of

---

477 See Riddell: Addressing Crimes Against International Law, p. 99.

478 See Waugh: Paul Kagame and Rwanda, p. 181.

479 See Drumbl: Punishment, Postgenocide, p. 1265; Riddell: Addressing Crimes Against International Law, p. 118.

480 See Mujawayo/Belhaddad: Auf der Suche nach Stéphanie, pp. 73ff.

481 See Elshtain: Politics and Forgiveness, p. 57.

482 See Schilling: Gegen das Vergessen, p. 113.

483 See Riddell: Addressing Crimes Against International Law, p. 100.

484 See Christopher J. Le Mon: Rwanda's Troubled Gacaca Courts, in: Human Rights Brief, Vol. 14 (2007) 2, in: http://www.wcl.american.edu/hrbrief/14/2lemon.pdf?rd=1 (23.03.2008), pp. 17f.

485 See Penal Reform International: From Camp to Hill, p. 14.

486 See Penal Reform International: Integrated Report on Gacaca Research and Monitoring, p. 23.

their imprisonment Tutsi this perception fuels ethnic mistrust.[487] Tutsis on the other hand doubt that the truth will be established through Gacaca as they feel the detainees are not speaking out and the general Hutu population is not interested in participating at Gacaca.[488]

Another problem with truth is that there often is not only one truth and especially in ethnically divided societies like Rwanda the quest for truth can even widen the divisions between the adversaries.[489] There is no consensus in Rwanda about who was killed and how numerous the killers were, which ethnic group suffered more, the history before the genocide and the tensions between the groups prior to 1994 and so on.[490] The short period of four years is a contested issue itself and cannot include all the above mentioned points. It leaves out a large part of Rwanda's history of violence and will therefore fail to establish the whole truth.[491] The biggest danger for reconciliation with respect to truth at Gacaca is the fact that only Hutu are accused while Tutsi who killed Hutu do not have to defend themselves at Gacaca. If a whole picture of all atrocities is to be established Tutsi need to be held accountable for their deeds as well. If the truth aired is simply a Tutsi truth that leaves out the Hutu standpoint, it will frustrate and alienate large parts of the population and not contribute to reconciliation. Unfortunately, this is happening.[492] People may want to talk about the crimes committed and lift the blanket of silence, but they want all crimes brought out to the open.[493]

Another obstacle to truth is of practical nature. After the genocide and war, residence patterns have shifted profoundly. Many survivors have emigrated.[494] The composition of the population is not the same as before and is acerbated by the fact that perpetrators do not return to their home communes out of fear of revenge.[495] Recent immigrants, mostly returnees from neighbouring countries, have not witnessed the genocide. Hutu on the other hand tend to withdraw from politics and are reluctant to accuse other Hutu.[496] These practical constraints coupled with the fact that memories begin to blur eight years after the atrocities occurred constitute a serious challenge for Gacaca, as witnesses are lacking to establish truth.[497] To conclude: Gacaca is theoretically a

487 See Drumbl: Punishment, Postgenocide, p. 1275.

488 See Riddell: Addressing Crimes Against International Law, p. 151.

489 See Zupan/Servaes: Transitional Justice and Dealing with the Past, p. 6.

490 See Daly: Between Punitive and Reconstructive Justice, p. 358.

491 See Sarkin: The Tension Between Justice and Reconciliation in Rwanda, p. 161.

492 See Corey/Joireman: Retributive Justice, p. 88.

493 See Wierzynska: Consolidating Democracy through Rwanda's Transitional Gacaca Courts, p. 1965.

494 See Gabisirege/Babalola: Perceptions About the Gacaca Law in Rwanda, p. 6.

495 See Wenke: Gacaca Rechtssprechung in Ruanda, p. 45.

496 See Daly: Between Punitive and Reconstructive Justice, p. 380.

497 See Wenke: Gacaca Rechtssprechung in Ruanda, p. 38.

good truth mechanism but the realities on the ground suggest that it is not able to live up to its expectations.

The Guilty Plea Procedure

The Rwandan government has responded to these constraints and established a guilty plea procedure to overcome the biggest obstacle in prosecutions, namely the lack of evidence.[498] Confessions are encouraged through the reduction of prison sentences which means that the accused can be reintegrated in the community quickly. It is hoped that the confessions will lead to forgiveness by the victims. To achieve this aim the Gacaca law asks the perpetrators to seek apology from the victims when they confess. Apologies were an integral part of the traditional Gacaca and serve as an important tool for reconciliation.[499] For the prisoners it makes sense to confess and reduce their sentence and many are ready to testify against other suspects. But the personal reasons of the accused do not really matter. The fact that the truth is aired through confessions is an integral part of restorative justice and an important contribution to reconciliation.[500] Therefore "the confession procedure is key to Gacaca's success in uncovering the truth."[501]

However, to confess a crime when the victim is present is considered an insult in Rwandan culture. As a consequence the ways in which confessions are brought forward are often perceived as arrogant by the victims.[502] For them, the monotone voice and the emotionless face of the accused are hard to bear, especially because that sharply contrasts the content of the confessions.[503] Another problem is that most accused do not share all their knowledge but only the parts someone might already know. When they feel safe that certain acts will not be uncovered they keep them to themselves. Consequently it is hard to uncover the whole truth.[504] Many of the killed have no killer yet as there are less confessions than victims. That puts a heavy burden on the relatives as they remain in the dark about the fate of their loved ones.[505] This is why many of the initial wave of confessions have been rejected by authorities claiming they were incomplete or did not tell the truth.[506]

---

498 See Vandeginste: Rwanda, p. 262.

499 See Graybill: Pardon, Punishment, and Amnesia, pp. 1123f.

500 See Tiemessen: After Arusha, p. 62

501 Riddell: Addressing Crimes Against International Law, p. 114.

502 See Penal Reform International: Integrated Report on Gacaca Research and Monitoring, p. 23.

503 See Mujawayo/Belhaddad: Auf der Suche nach Stéphanie, p. 85.

504 See Robert Walker: Rwanda Still Searching for Justice (04.03.2008), in: BBC News, in: http://news.bbc.co.uk/2/hi/africa/3557753.stm (14.06.2008), [Subsection 5].

505 See Hankel: Vergangenheit, die nicht ruhen darf, p. 8.

506 See Human Rights Watch: World Report 2007, p. 1.

Furthermore, forcing testimony in public at Gacaca risks producing false testimony.[507] Innocent people might confess to get out of prison. The provisional release of the confessed is another source of trouble. Many survivors think that they are released for good and lose hope in the Gacaca system. Additionally, the pressure created by the confession procedure and the fear of guilty people still at large that they might be implicated have brought back hatred, mistrust and threats to the hills. If families of inmates are threatened, the accused person is pressured into silence.[508] So the confession procedure might bring back the very hatred Gacaca seeks to erase. Still, it is Gacaca's best bet to become a success story and even if there are problems regarding the truthfulness of confessions at least part of the truth is aired, which clearly works towards the healing of survivors.

Healing and Gacaca

Victims need public recognition of their suffering, support, reparation and the truth to begin the healing process.[509] All this happens at Gacaca. Many feel that by telling their stories they can start to heal and re-enter into society.[510] However, the risk of re-traumatization and renewed hostility through Gacaca is evident.[511] This risk is especially grave as there are not sufficient counselling services available in Rwanda to cater for the victims at all Gacaca sessions.[512] Giving public testimony might be a relief for the victims but it does not address the individual struggles every one of them is fighting every day. Revealing is not automatically healing.[513] This is true all the more as the ambiance at Gacaca is often rather hostile and not as sympathetic to the victims as the sessions of the South African Truth and Reconciliation Commission.[514]
Despite these risks Gacaca is the most victim-centred form of justice Rwanda has to offer at the moment. The judgements on a local level made by local people help to empower victims.[515] Gacaca serves as a platform for victims

---

507 See Werchick: Prospects for Justice, [Subsection 10].

508 See Riddell: Addressing Crimes Against International Law, pp. 108f.

509 See Biggar: Making Peace or Doing Justice, p. 8.

510 See Shriver: Where and When in Political Life Is Justice Served by Forgiveness?, p. 30.

511 See Staub/Pearlman: Advancing Healing and Reconciliation, p. 228.

512 See Tiemessen: After Arusha, p. 64. Some international organizations provide psychosocial assistance in addition to Rwandan efforts but that is hardly enough; see for example DED-ZFD: Ziviler Friedensdienst Ruanda, in: http://ruanda.ded.de/cipp/ded/custom/pub/content,lang,1/oid,5910/ticket,g_u_e_s_t/~/Ziviler_Friedensdienst.html (14.06.08).

513 See Hamber: Does the Truth Heal?, p. 160.

514 See Riddell: Addressing Crimes Against International Law, p. 146.

515 See Drumbl: Punishment, Postgenocide, p. 1264.

and enables them to come together with the perpetrators and hear their apologies.[516] As victims play a crucial role for reconciliation, a victim-centred approach like Gacaca is a good tool to achieve reconciliation.[517] Certainly this positive judgement of Gacaca by various scholars draws on theoretical aspects of Gacaca. In theory Gacaca contributes to healing and pays a lot of attention to victims as crucial players in the reconciliation process. In practice, however, intimidation of survivors often occurs and the ambiance is rather unsupportive.[518] More has to be done to address these problems and judges should actively work against intimidation and mobbing to make Gacaca's potential fertile.

The question of reparation

As has been said before, reparation is important to victims' healing. Gacaca can be effectively used for that as the core element of traditional justice has always been reparation. Nowadays prisoners help to rebuild houses of genocide victims as reparation.[519] Work done by prisoners as part of their sentence also contributes to reparation on the level of society in general.[520] The amended Gacaca law therefore provides for an increased use of punishment through community service.[521] Problematic in that respect is the fact that "work as punishment" was frequently used in the colonial period and that it resembles the patron-client relationship of *ubuhake* explained in chapter 3. This could lead to the perception of Hutu that they are still the suppressed part of the population.[522] Survivors, on the other hand, turn away from Gacaca as in practice there are few material compensations.[523] In addition to material needs the problem of land – which is a major source of tension in overpopulated Rwanda with its shifted residence patterns – is not addressed at Gacaca.[524] Again, practical constraints in a poor country restrict the essentially great potential of Gacaca to contribute to reconciliation through reparation. If more resources became available, however, Gacaca could be a success.

---

516 See Zorbas: Reconciliation in Post-genocide Rwanda, p. 36.

517 See Zupan/Servaes: Transitional Justice and Dealing with the Past, p. 12.

518 See Mujawayo/Belhaddad: Auf der Suche nach Stéphanie, p. 67.

519 See Waugh: Paul Kagame and Rwanda, p. 183.

520 See Vandeginste: Rwanda, p. 276.

521 See Human Rights Watch: World Report 2008, p. 145.

522 See Penal Reform International: Research on Gacaca Report. Report IV "The Guilty Plea Procedure, Cornerstone of the Rwandan Justice System", Kigali/Paris 2003, p. 17.

523 See Penal Reform International: Integrated Report on Gacaca Research and Monitoring, p. 48.

524 See Nsengiyaremye: Zehn Jahre danach, p. 95.

The problem of overcrowded prisons and expedition of trials

Expedition of trials is one of the main goals of Gacaca and the courts can certainly be successful in executing quick justice.[525] It is the best mechanism to assure Rwandans that justice is being done in due time while conventional trials would take hundreds of years. The overcrowding of prisons, however, might not be alleviated through Gacaca. Even though it leads to the acquittal of perpetrators after they have confessed it also brings newly accused persons behind bars, as testimonies of inmates implicate new suspects.[526] Furthermore the courts have an unmanageable workload to carry[527] and are already far behind schedule.[528]

Reintegration through Gacaca

The reintegration of prisoners into their home communes is one of the restorative features of Gacaca.[529] It bears the chance that denial of the genocide becomes impossible as people come together to debate what happened. Shaming of *genocidaires* in the community, partly through Gacaca, can help to avoid future violence as it becomes an unacceptable option. Also, perpetrators can see with their own eyes what suffering they inflicted and that in turn might change their internal attitudes. While inside the prison it is easy to deny one's accountability. Back in the village this is no longer possible.[530] Reintegration brings all stakeholders together and the accused, victims, bystanders and the community in general have to face each other and create new bonds.[531] It is also a political and economic necessity as a country in ruins cannot afford to keep the majority of breadwinners in prison while the economy is in shambles. Furthermore, the inhumane prison conditions and the situation of the families of the accused can build up a desire for revenge.[532] There is no alternative to reintegration. But survivors as well as perpetrators understandably fear the return of *genocidaires* to the villages. For victims their worst nightmares become reality when they have to face the killers and live next door to them

---

525 See Hornberger: Rwandan Gacaca Courts in Crisis, p. 9.

526 See Daly: Between Punitive and Reconstructive Justice, pp. 375 and 383f.

527 See Wenke: Gacaca Rechtssprechung in Ruanda, p. 39.

528 See Tiemessen: After Arusha, p. 61.

529 See Gready: Reconceptualising Transitional Justice, p. 12.

530 See Drumbl: Punishment, Postgenocide, pp. 1261f.

531 See Wierzynska: Consolidating Democracy through Rwanda's Transitional Gacaca Courts, p. 1959.

532 See Schilling: Gegen das Vergessen, p. 132.

again. The prisoners fear the anger of survivors and wonder how the community will receive them.[533]

Fears of the population and the problem of mistrust

Gacaca aims at overcoming distrust and restoring relationships within communities.[534] Participants of a study conducted in 2001 stated that relationships have improved a lot but mistrust persists in Rwandan society between Hutu and Tutsi. Mistrust is more strongly felt by persons that have lost family members in the genocide or war and perceived as a major problem.[535] Fear and mistrust are greatest among survivors and released prisoners. The resulting intimidations and manipulations in the context of Gacaca endanger the whole project. Gacaca cannot operate in a climate of fear and insecurity.[536] The lack of trust in the Gacaca system itself became clear when 10.000 Rwandans fled the country out of fear of Gacaca when the jurisdictions started their work. The fact that a number of witnesses has been killed across the country certainly does not add to a feeling of security which is needed for Gacaca.[537] Consequently, if Gacaca is to overcome the mistrust within the population the authorities have to provide security and assure the Rwandans that Gacaca is beneficial rather than threatening for them.

Attitudes and participation of the population

When the Gacaca courts were established in 2001 the overall attitude of the population was positive. They set high hopes in the courts and expressed confidence that they would bring about reconciliation. People stated they were ready to participate and to give evidence.[538] In some prisons inmates already started their own Gacaca sessions, which once again proves the high support this justice mechanism enjoys in the Rwandan population.[539] The trust in Gacaca has waned over the years, however. Corruption, false accusations and faulty procedures have led to a decline in participation and trust.[540] People now often just attend the meetings without actively taking part in resolving

533 See Mujawayo/Belhaddad: Auf der Suche nach Stéphanie, pp. 127 and 163.
534 See Amstutz: Is Reconciliation Possible After Genocide?, p. 556.
535 See Gabisirege/Babalola : Perceptions About the Gacaca Law in Rwanda, pp. 7f.
536 See Penal Reform International: Integrated Report on Gacaca Research and Monitoring, p. 35.
537 See Le Mon: Rwanda's Troubled Gacaca Courts, p. 17.
538 See Gabisirege/Babalola : Perceptions About the Gacaca Law in Rwanda, p. 13.
539 See Penal Reform International: Integrated Report on Gacaca Research and Monitoring, p. 22.
540 See Human Rights Watch: World Report 2008, p. 145.

the cases.[541] As participation of the population is an absolute necessity, the government has to address the existing problems and fight corruption and false accusations actively.

Acknowledgement of guilt, apologies and forgiveness

Forgiveness can be generated between individuals if an individual offender apologizes to the victim.[542] Acknowledgement of guilt and of what happened is crucial for reconciliation.[543] Therefore the apology written in the Gacaca law is an important step in the right direction and shows the potential of Gacaca for reconciliation – on paper, that is.[544] Some encouraging cases have been recorded already where Hutu prisoners asked Tutsi for forgiveness and pleaded guilty, and the Tutsi in turn accepted the apology and visited the men in prison.[545]

However, forgiveness is often artificial at Gacaca. It is the key element of the process but if people feel pressured to forgive and reconcile by the authorities, the resulting reconciliation remains shallow and artificial.[546] Very few perpetrators make an individual attempt to ask forgiveness. Survivors feel they are pressured into forgiving even if the apologies are not sincere or perpetrators do not show repentance.[547] Many prisoners are not really sorry and fail to acknowledge their guilt. Instead they tend to blame others. The unwillingness of perpetrators to seek forgiveness and to admit their involvement seriously damages the Gacaca jurisdictions.[548] Survivors claim that letters from prisoners asking forgiveness are often cold, without repentance and acknowledgement of their own guilt. That makes it difficult for the victims to forgive.[549] The government should reduce pressure on the people and give them space to

541 See Oomen: Donor-Driven Justice, p. 904.

542 See Catherine Philpot/Matthew Hornsey: Asking Forgiveness for the Sins of Many. Does it Work?, in: American Psychological Association (ed.): Forgiveness. A Sampling of Research Results (Compiled by the American Psychological Association on the Occasion of the 59th Annual DPI/NGO Conference United Nations Headquarters, Midday Workshop "*Forgiveness: Partnering with the Enemy*"), Washington 2006, in: http://www.apa.org/international/un-forgive.pdf (12.01.2008), p. 22.

543 See Gready: Reconceptualising Transitional Justice, p. 7.

544 See Graybill: Pardon, Punishment, and Amnesia, p. 1124.

545 See Uvin/Mironko: Western and Local Approaches to Justice in Rwanda, p. 228.

546 See Richters/Dekker/De Jonge: Reconciliation in the Aftermath of Violent Conflict in Rwanda, p. 214.

547 See Penal Reform International: Integrated Report on Gacaca Research and Monitoring, p. 25.

548 See Riddell: Addressing Crimes Against International Law, pp. 112ff.

549 See Mujawayo/Belhaddad: Auf der Suche nach Stéphanie, p. 135.

reconcile. Admission of guilt is difficult but might be facilitated through the reintegration of prisoners that find denial impossible in the villages.

The issue of collective guilt[550]

Collective guilt is a big problem in the context of justice in Rwanda. There will be no reconciliation if all Hutu are labelled *genocidaires* and all Tutsi are accused of human rights violations during the war.[551] Hutu in Rwanda today fear they might be accused of crimes they did not commit while at the same time they do not receive justice for crimes committed against them.[552] Gacaca can help to individualize guilt and establish personal accountability through bringing individuals to court and discovering the truth about guilty and innocent.[553]

The question of ethnicity

Closely connected to collective guilt is the issue of ethnicity. Gacaca might be the most suitable form to bring the two groups together and create a shared account of history. Identities can be redefined through exchange.[554] But ethnicity also influences people's perceptions on justice and how they are treated by the judicial system. Gacaca can therefore also deepen ethnic divisions if one group feels disadvantaged by it.[555] If Gacaca only prosecutes Hutu and not RPF crimes committed during the war it simply confirms the group identities of victims and perpetrators and assigns collective guilt to Hutu. This does not enhance reconciliation but further widens the ethnic rift.[556] Consequently, this situation needs to be changed.

The contested impartiality of the courts: Fighting impunity?

Crimes committed by the RPF during the war or after they seized power are not subject to Gacaca jurisdictions. The government is of the opinion that these crimes are a product of war and therefore need to be addressed at military tribunals as opposed to crimes of genocide at Gacaca. In their view RPF/RPA elements are soldiers while the accused (Hutu) killers at Gacaca are

550 There is a big discussion on collective guilt and collective innocence among scholars that will not be outlined here as it is only a small aspect of the topic and not integral for this thesis.

551 See Lemarchand: Genocide in the Great Lakes, p. 11.

552 See Human Rights Watch: Killings in Eastern Rwanda, p. 13.

553 See Graybill: Pardon, Punishment, and Amnesia, p. 1124.

554 See Wenke: Gacaca Rechtssprechung in Ruanda, p. 46.

555 See Corey/Joireman: Retributive Justice, p. 89.

556 See Le Mon: Rwanda's Troubled Gacaca Courts, pp. 18f.

genocidaires. The crimes are not in the same league, they argue. This argument enforces the notion of victor's justice. And again the very politicisation of ethnicity comes into play that fuelled the genocide in 1994.[557] The RPF has investigated crimes committed by its soldiers and tried some of them.[558] But for the general population this is not visible. The double standard of prosecutions will inevitably further divide the country.[559] The refusal of the RPF to have crimes committed by the army tried at Gacaca leads to the denial of the genocide by Hutu and talk of a counter-genocide.[560] This is certainly highly problematic. Hutu suffered in the refugee camps without doubt and the RPF committed atrocities. But it would be dangerous to equate the genocide with the war crimes. As memories become blurred the extent and scope of the genocide can quickly become forgotten. The RPF must not let that happen by refusing their atrocities to be investigated by Gacaca.[561]

There will be no reconciliation if Tutsi are not tried as well for their crimes. Justice in the current form is victor's justice and perceived as revenge by Hutu.[562] It is quite common for a formerly victimized ethnic group to reject the notion of their own guilt, and tend to refuse to admit that their group committed crimes, too.[563] But participation at Gacaca is dropping as survivors of RPF atrocities are neither acknowledged nor compensated. Gacaca is being perceived as victor's justice and this will most likely make the whole exercise fail despite the many advantages Gacaca provides. Deterrence and prevention of future violence will not succeed.[564] Fighting impunity was one of the main goals of Gacaca stated by the government. Theoretically the massive prosecution efforts can achieve that goal as people see that killing no longer goes unpunished. But the culture of impunity is not eroded, it persists with the RPF crimes.[565]

Interfering with local justice: The influence of politics

The political system in a transition period influences justice in the short run, but also has important implications for justice in the long haul.[566] There are

557 See Tiemessen: After Arusha, pp. 69f.
558 See Des Forges: Leave None to Tell the Story, p. 733.
559 See Richters/Dekker/De Jonge: Reconciliation in the Aftermath of Violent Conflict in Rwanda, p. 206.
560 See Zorbas: Reconciliation in Post-genocide Rwanda, p. 41.
561 See Mackintosh: Rwanda. Beyond Ethnic Conflict, p. 747.
562 See Corey/Joireman: Retributive Justice, pp. 86 and 88.
563 See Barsalou: Trauma and Transitional Justice in Divided Societies, p. 7.
564 See Riddell: Addressing Crimes Against International Law, pp. 124f.
565 See Longman/Rutagengwa: Memory, Identity and Community in Rwanda, p. 167.
566 See Pankhurst: Issues of Justice and Reconciliation in Complex Political Emergencies, p. 253.

some positive points, for example the focus on those prisoners that have not yet confessed in the Gacaca pilot phase. That helped to improve the image of Gacaca courts as an impartial justice mechanism that presumes the innocence of the accused.[567] Furthermore the presidential communiqué in 2003 on the provisional release of up to 40.000 confessed prisoners is a positive point in case. It shows the goodwill of the government to abstain from the notion of collective guilt and can help to reconcile population and government.[568]

The downside appears to be greater, however. There is a great lack of trust between the population and the government in Rwanda which hardly surprises given the authoritarian grip on power by the RPF described in chapter 4.[569] The political realities are reflected in the Gacaca jurisdictions and can be observed at the sessions. As most Hutu and even genocide survivors do not trust the government and feel it does not represent them they tend to be suspicious about Gacaca as well. As much as people endorse this traditional mechanism and have showed positive attitudes towards it, the fact that the new Gacaca courts are a government project is likely to damage their originally positive image within the population. Furthermore, the political realities of a Tutsi minority government that suppresses ethnicity (see chapters 3 and 4) and divides the population into perpetrators (Hutu) and victims (Tutsi) will do little to promote reconciliation at Gacaca. Instead, Hutu fear that justice merely masks Tutsi hunger for power. The ongoing exclusion of Hutu from power in Rwanda reinforces that perception.[570] The Rwandan government successfully has played out a dichotomy between the good guys – being the Tutsi – and the bad guys – being the Hutu. This dichotomy undermines justice and leads to a politicisation of justice at every level which endangers the credibility of justice in general, and of the supposedly communal Gacaca justice in particular.[571] Even the survivors' organization Ibuka has pointed out the political manipulation of justice. This is an interesting fact as Gacaca was set up to a great extent to benefit survivors.[572]

The exclusion of RPF crimes from Gacaca enforces the perception that Gacaca is less about bringing justice but about tightening Tutsi grip on power. The government uses Gacaca to cling to power, and the population is aware of that. They feel it is their civil duty to attend Gacaca sessions. It would be

---

567 See Penal Reform International: Integrated Report on Gacaca Research and Monitoring, p. 38.

568 See Penal Reform International: Research on Gacaca Report, p. 11.

569 See Hofmeier: Soziokulturelle Kurzanalyse Ruanda, p. 19.

570 See Wierzynska: Consolidating Democracy through Rwanda's Transitional Gacaca Courts, pp. 1937 and 1963.

571 See Betts: Should Approaches to Post-Conflict Justice and Reconciliation Be Determined Globally, Nationally or Locally?, p. 749.

572 See International Crisis Group: Rwanda at the End of the Transition, p. 12.

important for the people to own the process, especially as it is a community project. Instead, Gacaca is a government enforced mechanism and perceived as such by the population. Obedience rather than enthusiasm and ownership is the primary driving force of participation. This runs counter to the ideals of localized, traditional justice. Instead, the observation of the jurisdictions by the state and the presence of officials at the sessions strengthen an already centralist state. The communities are asked to participate in justice, but the elites still do the thinking for the ordinary peasants.[573]

Extremely damaging for the whole process has also been the increasing recourse to force by local authorities to ensure participation at Gacaca. Instead of examining the reasons for dwindling attendance officials force the people to attend Gacaca. Forced attendance paralyzes testimony and will not help in the search for truth. To the contrary, it causes people's confidence in Gacaca to crumble.[574] Local power dynamics are often rather part of the problem than part of the solution and this seems to be the case at Gacaca, too. Autocratic and authoritarian government behaviour is a grave risk especially as power holders seek to influence local mechanisms.[575] The combination of a state-imposed reconciliation process, a Tutsi ethnocracy and politicised victor's justice is a highly explosive mix and can lead the whole Gacaca experiment to fail.[576] Political manipulation possibly leads to mistrust, hatred, and ethnic tensions – the very outcome Gacaca seeks to avoid.[577] Unity and reconciliation can become mere propaganda as the practice at Gacaca differs more and more from the model of traditional, local and community-owned justice.[578]

Can Gacaca strengthen democracy?

Opinions on this topic are highly divided. One side holds that Gacaca cannot be a forum for democratic dialogue due to the tight grip on it by authorities that use the courts to accuse their opponents of divisionism and turn them into an area for their own political interests.[579] Others argue that Gacaca will help to develop a civic culture through dialogue and will therefore provide a

573 See Oomen: Donor-Driven Justice, pp. 905f.

574 See Penal Reform International: Integrated Report on Gacaca Research and Monitoring, p. 40.

575 See Gready: Reconceptualising Transitional Justice, pp. 9 and 14.

576 See Tiemessen: After Arusha, p. 64.

577 See Wenke: Gacaca Rechtssprechung in Ruanda, p. 41.

578 See Gerd Hankel: Über den schwierigen Versuch der Vergangenheitsaufarbeitung in Ruanda, in: Jörg Calliess (ed.): Zehn Jahre danach. Völkermord in Ruanda, Loccum 2005 (Dokumentation einer Tagung der evangelischen Akademie Loccum vom 5. bis 7. März 2004), pp. 108f.

579 See for example Le Mon: Rwanda's Troubled Gacaca Courts, p. 19.

grassroots force towards democracy that overcomes the top-down manner of Rwandan politics. In this view Gacaca is the only possible birthplace for democracy in Rwanda. Even if the courts cannot bring about justice and reconciliation, they can move Rwanda towards democracy.[580] In turn, if democracy is the best system to manage conflict and achieve reconciliation as stated in the introduction[581], all hope would not be lost for reconciliation in the long run.

5.3.3 Assessment of Gacaca's contribution to reconciliation

Le Mon sums up the three common assessments of the Gacaca experiment in Rwanda. The negative view regards the jurisdictions as an inadequate means to deliver justice to Rwanda, especially as it violates due process rules and human rights. The positive stance celebrates Gacaca as the best new invention in transitional justice that fosters democracy and strengthens reconciliation. The middle ground accepts the faults of the mechanism but concludes that given the political, economic and social conditions in Rwanda after the genocide the Gacaca jurisdictions are the best and only possible attempt for justice and reconciliation at present.[582] In Rwanda, there are no perfect and easy solutions.[583] Rating the success of Gacaca is likely to be relative. It cannot be measured against ideal situations but has to keep the real alternatives in mind.[584]

The assessment in this chapter has shown several things: the traditional character of the courts and the involvement of the community in the quest for justice are promising features of Gacaca that can help to rebuild broken ties between people through a mechanism that is familiar to them. It has much more potential to establish truth about the genocide than conventional court sessions through its confession and guilty-plea procedures. It is the most victim centred form of Rwanda's judicial approaches and offers the possibility of reparations. As confessions allow for the release of prisoners, reintegration as an integral part of restorative justice becomes possible. Acknowledgement of guilt and apologies, important for survivors to grant forgiveness, are part of Gacaca and can foster reconciliation. Last but not least the burden of collective guilt can be lifted from Hutu as individual responsibility is established in the Gacaca sessions.

---

580 See for example Wierzynska: Consolidating Democracy through Rwanda's Transitional Gacaca Courts, pp. 1953 and 1957.

581 See Bloomfield: The Context of Reconciliation, p. 10.

582 See Le Mon: Rwanda's Troubled Gacaca Courts, p. 16.

583 See Uvin/Mironko: Western and Local Approaches to Justice in Rwanda, p. 229.

584 See Forsberg: The Philosophy and Practice of Dealing with the Past, p. 79.

There are practical constraints on the ground, however. Mistrusts and fears persist. Prisoners are afraid to be reintegrated into their communities, and survivors fear their release. Gacaca sessions are accompanied by mobbing and intimidation of victims. Reparations are often not possible due to lack of resources. The prison overcrowding might not be eased as new accusations bring more people behind bars. The most worrying fact is the dropping participation at Gacaca. As much as people welcomed the introduction of Gacaca, the situation has changed now and Gacaca cannot work without the testimonies of villagers.

5.4 Dealing with the past and reconciliation in Rwanda through transitional justice: Overall assessment of all three approaches

The impact of transitional justice is extremely difficult to evaluate.[585] Mechanisms that aim at peace and reconciliation through truth and justice do not necessarily lead to these outcomes. Nor do they automatically restore relationships and trust in societies.[586] Chapter five has examined the impact of the ICTR, the national court system and the Gacaca jurisdictions on reconciliation in Rwanda with the biggest emphasis laid on the Gacaca courts. It has been made clear how important meting out justice in the Rwandan context is given the culture of impunity and the desire of the population for justice. The conclusion of a compared analysis of different forms of justice is the following: The ICTR and the national court system have produced neither justice nor truth for Rwandans. By excluding remorse from its proceedings, conventional retributive justice does little to alleviate the victims' pain and mend relationships between victims and perpetrators. The characteristics of conventional judicial approaches to arrive at justice are ill-suited for Rwanda.

Gacaca, on the other hand, shows all the distinctive features needed for reconciliation and is culturally familiar with Rwandans. Theoretically, it is an ideal solution for dealing with the past in Rwanda. Practical constraints and the interference of politics limit its ability to promote peace and reconciliation, however. Alana Thiemessen's assessment of the potential of transitional justice in general therefore seems to adequately sum up the complexity of justice and reconciliation in Rwanda:

"The most important lesson from Rwanda's reconciliation process is that the path from justice to reconciliation is not necessarily linear. In reality, this path is conditioned by two important factors: the relationship between victim and aggressor as well as the form of power that justice flows from. In Rwanda's

585 See Barsalou: Trauma and Transitional Justice in Divided Societies, p. 2.

586 See Zupan/Servaes: Transitional Justice and Dealing with the Past, p. 5.

case, these factors leave us with grave concerns for the ability of any kind of justice to contribute to reconciliation."[587]

This leaves us with the paradox that justice is urgently needed for reconciliation in Rwanda, but might not be possible in practice.

587 Tiemessen: After Arusha, p. 71.

6 Conclusion

Reconciliation and healing wounds takes generations. Fifteen years after the genocide it is therefore too early to judge whether reconciliation has been achieved in Rwanda. It can be analyzed, however, if the current conditions in Rwanda are favourable for future reconciliation.

Chapter 3 has shown that the conflict in Rwanda is ethnic in nature. Two opposing ethnic groups have developed in the course of the nineteenth and twentieth centuries, nurtured by the Belgian colonizers. The 1994 genocide and the refugee crisis that followed have deepened the divisions between the adversaries. They nurtured the respective myths circulating within in the groups and strengthened their identities as victims of violence, justifying future violence against the opponent. These conflicting perceptions on history, the development of ethnicity, suffering and the political power struggle have a grave impact on reconciliation, as only overcoming the different versions in favour of a shared account of history can pave the way for future peace. As long as each group clings to its myths violence will always be a justifiable option to defend oneself. Reconciliation therefore requires abandoning biased, ethnically interpreted truths and acknowledgement of the fact that Hutu and Tutsi are above all humans and Rwandans.

Ethnicity is not the only defining principle in Rwandan society today. Various subgroups exist as chapter 3.3.1 has shown. But the exclusion of the Hutu group from power and wealth sharpens ethnic differences and leads to a strong identification with one ethnic group rather than a subgroup. People fall back into the stereotypes of oppressor and oppressed that existed before independence. The government on the other hand has replaced ethnicity by the concept of Rwandanness. However, the banning of ethnicity does not work. Preventing the population from addressing ethnic discrimination just sends ethnicity underground. The goal of national unity is worthwhile and potentially encouraging for reconciliation as it aims at overcoming the ethnic conflict and creating a single Rwandan citizenship that does not need to use violence to compete in the political sphere. However, the authoritarian government style of a minority party – the RPF – directly contradicts the idea of equality of all Rwandans. Rwanda has experienced a Tutsification of power and wealth. Hutu are systematically excluded and persecuted under the disguise of divisionism. The government uses the military and intelligence to mete out the opposition. Leading Hutu members of the RPF have shown their discontent with military dictator Kagame by fleeing the country; genocide survivors have followed their example. As much as the RPF is trying to uphold the multiethnic façade, the population is well aware of the fact that it is ruled by a Tutsi oligarchy. This repeats the colonial pattern when Tutsi suppressed Hutu with the help of the Belgians. The minority RPF cannot be a government for all Rwandans, especially from a Hutu perspective. The repressive style of politics thus rather strengthens the circulating myths about victimization than contributing to a united country that is able to reconcile.

The political regime effectively dominates the reconciliation discourse and at the same time inhibits reconciliation. It tries to impose a government reading of history and ways to memorize the genocide top-down. But people form their own narratives privately. Oppression produces violent opposition. There is a good chance that Hutu will sharpen their machetes again if political space is not liberalized and discontent allowed. Governments cannot impose reconciliation. They can enhance it through certain measures but in the end it is a personal process that needs to be achieved by the population. In Rwanda the government applies force instead of encouraging reconciliation programmes. But the population does not accept the imposition of a RPF version of history. Rather, people tend to withdraw into the private sphere and continue to teach their children old antagonistic and divisive myths.

The RPF ideology undermines reconciliation efforts and long term stability for the country. Anger and frustration are growing among Hutu and explaining ethnicity away strengthens tensions in a society clearly still marked by notions of ethnic differences. The situation today resembles the pre-genocide period. The authoritarian regime has produced silences and behaviour patterns that will likely lead to violence again. Tensions are boiling latently. The system of government and the manipulation of ethnicity, this time not through direct encouragement of hatred but through banning ethnicity to mask minority rule, are a grim reminder of the policy under the Habyarimana regime. Furthermore, impunity for the current government persists. History has shown that whenever a group in Rwanda is denied political representation and a fair share of power, it turns to violent means to change the situation. This danger clearly exists once more today.

Dealing with the past in Rwanda through justice must be analyzed under these premises. The central question asked in the introduction of this thesis was whether judicial strategies of dealing with the past can contribute to reconciliation in Rwanda. The record to date is mixed. Potentially justice is a key ingredient of reconciliation in any country, as chapter 2 has shown, and in Rwanda in particular, as explained in chapter 5.1.2. Ending the culture of impunity is a necessity in a country that has been characterized by outbursts of violence for decades, which have always gone unpunished. Furthermore, healing of victims can only start when perpetrators are brought to justice and acknowledge their guilt. Justice can also bring about another crucial element of reconciliation – truth. It helps victims to achieve closure and lifts the burden

of collective guilt from the Hutu population. That in turn helps the whole society to reconcile and build new trustful relationships.
The first response to the genocide has been the ICTR erected by the international community. This thesis argues that the tribunal has failed on all accounts. By bringing only a small fraction of the known prime *genocidaires* to court it has not been able to fulfil the Rwandan need for swift justice. Following the logic of classic retributive justice it has not established truth about 1994. To the contrary, denial and claims of a double genocide have characterized the behaviour of the defendants much more than admission of guilt and remorse. Furthermore, concentrating on individuals neglects the underlying causes of the genocide and does not lead to an understanding of the deep-rooted hatred that allowed ethnic violence to reach the proportions it did in 1994.
Neither group of the conflict has been interested in the outcome of the ICTR. Hutu extremists failed to acknowledge their guilt and demanded the prosecution of RPF crimes while the RPF refused to allow investigations into their own abuses. Instead of mutual understanding the court has produced an even greater confrontation of the extremists on both sides. For the Rwandan communities the ICTR has been irrelevant. Ordinary citizens do not understand the complex mechanism of international retributive justice. Thus, it has not contributed to the restoration of relationships within the communities in Rwanda or fostered reconciliation and forgiveness. The mandate of the ICTR will end this year and an evaluation is therefore possible now. The international answer to the genocide has maybe contributed to the development of international law, but failed to contribute to reconciliation in Rwanda. It is highly unlikely that this judgement will change in the future.
The national response to the genocide is characterized by a hardly veiled system of victor's justice. It does not contribute to a full picture of all atrocities committed in Rwanda in 1994 and beyond as it fails to prosecute RPF crimes. Official truths and politicized justice are the order of the day. Hutu are excluded from the judiciary. Tutsi judges prosecute Hutu *genocidaires.* Crimes against Hutu go largely unpunished. Therefore the national courts serve the aim of revenge rather than justice. The authoritarian government makes sure that only their version of history is established by the courts and not the full truth about Rwanda's history of violence. Neither truth nor justice has been achieved by the Rwandan courts to date.
Politicised justice and overcrowded prisons fuel ethnic tensions. Instead of restoring relationships in the communities it strains them, as Hutu families suffer under the burden of imprisoned family members and blame their Tutsi neighbours for the acts of the regime. Apart from that the slow pace of justice poses a serious threat to reconciliation. If reconciliation needs acknowledg-

ments by perpetrators and of victims, the fact that it will take hundreds of years to hear all cases is highly problematic. Victims cannot wait for acknowledgement forever, and they want to know the fate of their relatives now. Only if they hear the perpetrators' confessions and the verdicts of the court they can grant forgiveness as forgiveness is connected to admission of guilt in Rwandan culture. For a lot of victims it will be too late if the courts continue to hear cases at the current slow rate. National trials rather inhibit reconciliation at present. If reforms are pursued and the regime stops to interfere with justice there is a chance that trials could contribute to reconciliation in the future, however. This thesis has explained the benefits of retributive justice. If properly applied, trials can establish individual guilt and exonerate the greater share of the Hutu population of collective guilt as well as ending impunity. Unfortunately, the prospects for the future look rather grim if the RPF does not abandon its authoritarian path.

The Gacaca jurisdictions differ from the other approaches profoundly. First, they are a traditional Rwandan mechanism, although altered by the government to serve the new challenge of judging crimes of genocide, and are accepted as such by the population. They can therefore be deemed an example of African justice. Furthermore they are a form of local justice as opposed to international and national trials that are alien in procedure and far removed from daily life experiences of the general peasant population. They involve the communities directly in meting out justice and therefore bear the chance that people own the process. Third, they carry much more restorative features than the purely retributive trials inside Rwanda and in Arusha. It has been shown that the Gacaca jurisdictions have retributive competences that differ from the traditional model. Nevertheless restorative elements dominate: Confessions enable the establishment of truth, the acknowledgement of guilt and the reintegration of perpetrators into the communities. It is the most victim-centred form of justice Rwanda has to offer. The demand of victims for apologies is fulfilled by the inclusion of apologies in the Gacaca law. This provides hope that forgiveness will be granted by the victims eventually.

The question if Gacaca can develop a democratic culture in Rwanda, on the other hand, is hard to answer. At the moment it seems that the degree of authoritarianism does not allow for democratic movements in Rwanda. But if the pressure starts to crack, Gacaca as a model can certainly help to foster democracy through its described advantages and build a local grass roots movement towards a more democratic society. It certainly can empower communities to make their own decisions and learn that they do not always need state structures to tell them what to do.

The most promising feature of Gacaca is the involvement of the communities. If the aim of justice is the restoration of ruptured ties between Rwandans, working together for justice and discussing what has happened during the genocide can restore the social fabric of Rwandan society. The population is forced to solve problems in a judicial setting instead of using violence. Mutual understanding can develop as stories of victimization are shared and Rwandans realize that they all have become victims through the never ending cycles of violence in their country. This understanding is a prerequisite for reconciliation. While it is easy to hate another group after being exposed to hate propaganda and enemy images, mutual trust developed through direct interaction can provide the grounds for peaceful resolution of conflicts in the future. Political manipulation of ethnicity has been the order of the day throughout Rwanda's history. At Gacaca people can discover that their opponents are human beings like themselves and resist calls for violence by their leaders.

To conclude: Gacaca, as a traditional and restorative mechanism, bears a lot of hope for reconciliation and a transition to democracy. It combines all aspects identified as important for reconciliation in chapter 2, namely rebuilding relationships and communities, working for a shared future, acknowledgment of victims' suffering and perpetrators' guilt, healing of victims and forgiveness, truth and justice. It is therefore in the author's opinion an ideal vehicle for reconciliation if it adheres to these restorative elements.

However, political interference with community justice is the biggest threat to Gacaca at present. It is the firm belief of the author that the current political system with its oppression tactics, its refusal to introduce democracy, its ethnocratic character, its human rights abuses and its political manipulation of justice will cause the Gacaca experiment to fail. As much as Gacaca is a suitable mechanism for reconciliation on paper, the biased system of victor's justice erected by the RPF will reinforce the importance of ethnicity and deepen the ethnic divide. Unfortunately, the Rwandan government tends to stress the retributive aspects of Gacaca and alters its traditional structure to an extent that the population does not accept. It interferes with local justice and does not leave it to the population to solve their problems. Instead, it creates further tensions by refusing to let RPF atrocities be discussed at Gacaca. Instead of acknowledging all victims it regards only Tutsi as victims and Hutu as perpetrators. It inhibits the establishment of truth by Gacaca courts through repression and accusation of divisionism. It will contribute to the perception that Gacaca is the same partial victor's justice as the conventional trials. In short, all positive aspects of Gacaca that could lead to truth, reconciliation and trust, are threatened to evaporate under the pressure of the authorities.

All hope is not lost. If Gacaca is a theoretically good judicial approach to foster reconciliation in Rwanda, a change of government could make its potential fertile. If the government realizes that a minority dictatorship is not feasible in Rwanda and will lead to renewed violence, Gacaca could be revived under new auspices. It would be crucial that RPF atrocities are included in the courts' mandate and that the categories of Hutu perpetrators and Tutsi victims be changed. If that happened Gacaca might very well achieve reconciliation.

Justice in Rwanda can contribute to reconciliation. It must be traditional, restorative, "African" justice, however, and therefore Gacaca is much better suited to achieve this goal than the ICTR and the national courts that so far have rather inhibited reconciliation. Four years after the launch of Gacaca it is too early to give an answer whether Gacaca has succeeded. But dealing with the past is at an important crossroads in Rwanda now. There is a chance that Rwanda can bury its divided past and create a shared future. Reconciliation has occurred at times. But without democracy, human rights, equality and equal political representation of all ethnic groups stability and peace will not prevail. Rwanda will return to violence once more and fall back into the darkness.

7 Bibliography

Primary Sources: Official Documents and Interviews

British Broadcasting Cooperation: BBC Interview with Paul Kagame, in: http://www.gov.rw/government/president/interviews/2001/gacaca.html (13.06.2008).

European Commission: European Commission Welcomes Abolition of the Death Penalty in Rwanda (26.07.2007), in: http://europa.eu/rapid/pressReleasesAction.do?reference=IP/07/1183&format=HTML&aged=1&language=EN&guiLanguage=en (16.03.2008).

Organic Law N° 40/2000 of 26/01/2001 Setting up "Gacaca Jurisdictions" and Organizing Prosecutions for Offences Constituting the Crime of Genocide or Crimes Against Humanity Committed between October 1, 1990 and December 31, 1994, Kigali 2001.

Organic Law N° 28/2006 of 27/06/2006 Organic Law Modifying and Complementing Organic Law n° 16/2004 of 19/06/2004 Establishing the Organisation, Competence and Functioning of Gacaca Courts Charged With Prosecuting and Trying the Perpetrators of the Crime of Genocide and Other Crimes Against Humanity, Committed Between October 1, 1990 and December 31, 1994, Kigali 2006.

Rwanda Government: Rwandan Government List of Genocide Suspects, in: http://www.gov.rw/government/category1.htm (12.06.2008).

United Nations Security Council: Security Council Resolution 955 on 8th November 1994, in: http://daccessdds.un.org/doc/UNDOC/GEN/N95/140/97/PDF/N9514097.pdf?OpenElement (16.12.2007).

Deutscher Entwicklungsdienst/Ziviler Friedensdienst (DED-ZFD): Strategische Planung des Zivilen Friedensdienstes in Ruanda 2007-2012, Kigali 2006.

Deutscher Entwicklungsdienst/Ziviler Friedensdienst (DED-ZFD): Ziviler Friedensdienst Ruanda, in: http://ruanda.ded.de/cipp/ded/custom/pub/content,lang,1/oid,5910/ticket,g_u_e_s_t/~/Ziviler_Friedensdienst.html (14.06.08).

Primary Sources: Reports

Amnesty International: World Report 2007, London 2007, in: http://thereport.amnesty.org/document/15 (13.03.2008).

Bertelsmann Stiftung: Bertelsmann Transformation Index 2008. Rwanda Country Report, Gütersloh 2008, in: http://www.bertelsmann-transformation-index.de/fileadmin/pdf/Gutachten_BTI_2008/ESA/Rwanda.pdf (30.06.2008).

Freedom House: Freedom House Index. Rwanda 2007, Washington/New York 2007, in: http://www.freedomhouse.org/template.cfm?page=22&year=2007&country=7259 (30.06.2008).

Human Rights Watch: Uprooting the Rural Poor in Rwanda. Reconciliation, New York et al. 2001, in:

http://www.hrw.org/reports/2001/rwanda/rwnvilg-12.htm#P1036_156804 (02.05.2008).

Human Rights Watch: World Report 2007, New York et al. 2007, in: http://www.hrw.org/wr2k7/wr2007master.pdf (16.05.2007).

Human Rights Watch: World Report 2008, New York et al. 2008, in: http://hrw.org/wr2k8/pdfs/wr2k8_web.pdf (16.05.2008).

Human Rights Watch: Killings in Eastern Rwanda. No. 1, New York et al. 2007, in: http://www.hrw.org/backgrounder/africa/rwanda0107/rwanda0107web.pdf (16.05.2008).

International Crisis Group: Rwanda at the End of the Transition. A Necessary Political Liberalisation, Nairobi/Brüssel 2002 (International Crisis Group Africa Report No 53), in: http://www.crisisgroup.org/library/documents/report_archive/A400817_13112002.pdf (02.01.2008).

Penal Reform International: Research on Gacaca Report. Report IV "The Guilty Plea Procedure, Cornerstone of the Rwandan Justice System", Kigali/Paris 2003.

Penal Reform International: Research Report on the Gacaca. Report VI. From Camp to Hill, the Reintegration of Released Prisoners, Paris/Kigali 2004.

Penal Reform International: Integrated Report on Gacaca Research and Monitoring. Pilot

Phase January 2002 – December 2004, London/Kigali 2005.

United Nations Development Programme: Human Development Index. Going Beyond Income. Rwanda, New York 2007, in: http://hdrstats.undp.org/countries/country_fact_sheets/cty_fs_RWA.html (30.06.2008).

Books

Assefa, Hizkias: The Meaning of Reconciliation, in: European Centre for Conflict Prevention, in: http://www.gppac.net/documents/pbp/part1/2_reconc.htm (13.03.2008).

Barsalou, Judy: Trauma and Transitional Justice in Divided Societies, Washington D.C. 2005 (USIP Special Report Nr. 135).

Bächler, Günther: Violence Through Environmental Discrimination, Dordrecht et al. 1999 (Social Indicators Research Series Volume 2).

Becker, David: Ohne Hass keine Versöhnung. Das Trauma der Verfolgten, Freiburg 1992.

Braithwaite, John: Restorative Justice and Responsive Regulation, Oxford/New York 2002.

Brounéus, Karen: Reconciliation. Theory and Practice for Development Cooperation, Stockholm 2003 (Swedish International Development Cooperation Agency).

Brounéus, Karen: Reconciliation and Development, Berlin 2007 (FES Dialogue on Globalization. Occasional Papers Berlin Nr. 36).

Collier, Paul/Elliott, V.L./Hegre, Harvard/Hoeffler, Anke/Reynal-Querol, Marta/Sambanis, Nicholas: Breaking the Conflict Trap. Civil War and Development Policy, Washington D.C. 2003 (World Bank Policy Research Reports).

Chrétien, Jean-Pierre: The Great Lakes of Africa. Two Thousand Years of History, New York 2003.

Dallaire, Roméo: Shake Hands With the Devil. The Failure of Humanity in Rwanda, London 2004.

Des Forges, Alison: Leave None to Tell the Story. Genocide in Rwanda, New York/Paris 1999.

Des Forges, Alison: Kein Zeuge darf überleben. Der Genozid in Ruanda, Hamburg 2002.

Gabisirege, Simon/Babalola, Stella: Perceptions About the Gacaca Law in Rwanda. Evidence from a Multi-Method Study, Baltimore 2001 (Special Publication No. 19 John Hopkins

University School of Public Health), in : http://www.jhuccp.org/pubs/sp/19/English/19.pdf (12.06.3008).

Goodman, David: Fault Lines. Journeys Into the New South Africa, Berkeley et al. 1999.

Gourevitch, Philip: Wir möchten Ihnen mitteilen, daß wir morgen mit unseren Familien umgebracht werden. Berichte aus Ruanda, Berlin 1999.

Guillot, Philippe/Minear, Larry: Soldiers to the Rescue. Humanitarian Lessons from Rwanda, Paris 1996.

Hanf, Theodor: Die politische Bedeutung ethnischer Gegensätze in Ruanda und Burundi, Freiburg 1964 (Materialien des Arnold Bergstraesser Instituts für Kulturwissenschaftliche Forschung).

Hofmeier, Rolf: Soziokulturelle Kurzanalyse Ruanda, Hamburg 2005.

Johnstone, Gerry: Restorative Justice. Ideas, Values, Debates, Portland 2005.

Lederach, John Paul: Building Peace. Sustainable Reconciliation in Divided Societies, 7th edition, Washington D.C. 2006.

Lehmann, Jörg: Thesenpapier zur Trauma-Arbeit im Kontext des Zivilen Friedensdienstes, insbesondere bei Versöhnungsprozessen, Bonn 2007 (Thesenpapier des Referats P10 im DED).

Lunn, Jon: The African Great Lakes Region. An End to Conflict?, London 2006 (House of Commons Library Research Paper 06/51), in: http://www.parliament.uk/commons/lib/research/rp2006/rp06-051.pdf (16.12.2007).

Mamdani, Mahmood: When Victims Become Killers. Colonialism, Nativism, and the Genocide in Rwanda, 3rd edition, Princeton 2002.

Minow, Martha: Between Vengeance and Forgiveness. Facing History after Genocide and Mass Violence, Boston 1998.

Mujawayo, Esther/Belhaddad, Souad: Auf der Suche nach Stéphanie. Ruanda zwischen Versöhnung und Verweigerung, Wuppertal 2007.

National Unity and Reconciliation Commission/Gesellschaft für technische Zusammenarbeit: NURC-GTZ Conference on the Presentation of the Grassroots Consultation and Evaluation Report. Kigali, Hotel des Milles Collines 25th of July 2002, Kigali 2002, in: www.grandlacs.net/doc/2968.pdf (10.02.2008).

Newbury, Catherine: The Cohesion of Oppression. Clientship and Ethnicity in Rwanda. 1860-1960, New York 1988.

Prunier, Gérard: The Rwanda Crisis 1959-1994. History of a Genocide, London 1995.

Riddell, Jennifer G.: Addressing Crimes Against International Law. Rwanda's Gacaca in Practice, Aberdeen 2005 (A Thesis Presented for the Degree of LL.M at the University of Aberdeen).

Saeger, Olivia: The Importance of Political Elites. Comparative Case Study of South Africa and Rwanda, Haverford 2007, in: http://thesis.haverford.edu/dspace/bitstream/10066/1035/1/2007SaegerO.pdf (19.05.2008).

Santayana, George: Life of Reason or The Phases of Human Progress. By George Santayana 2, London 1905.

Scheen, Thomas: Der Kongo und Ruanda. Konflikte in der Region der großen Seen, Bonn 2004 (Friedrich Ebert Stiftung Analyse), in: http://library.fes.de/pdf-files/id/02121.pdf (16.12.2007).

Schilling, Sandrine: Gegen das Vergessen. Justiz, Wahrheitsfindung und Versöhnung nach dem Genozid in Ruanda durch Mechanismen traditioneller Justiz. Gacaca Gerichte, Frankfurt am Main 2005.

Strizek, Helmut: Ruanda und Burundi von der Unabhängigkeit zum Staatszerfall. Studien über eine gescheiterte Demokratie im afrikanischen Zwischenseengebiet, München 1996.

Strizek, Helmut: Kongo, Zaire – Ruanda – Burundi. Stabilität durch erneute Militärherrschaft? Studie zur „neuen Ordnung" in Zentralafrika, München 1998.

Strizek, Helmut: Zur Lage der Menschenrechte in Ruanda. Leben nach dem Völkermord, Aachen 2003.

Stroh, Alexander: Legitimation allein durch Entwicklung? Das Beispiel Ruanda, Hamburg 2007 (GIGA Focus Afrika Nr. 11).

Teitel, Ruti G.: Transitional Justice, Oxford/New York 2000.

Tutu, Desmond: No Future Without Forgiveness, London et al. 1999.

Waugh, Colin: Paul Kagame and Rwanda. Power, Genocide and the Rwandan Patriotic Front, Jefferson 2004.

Zupan, Natascha/Servaes, Sylvia: Transitional Justice and Dealing with the Past, Bonn 2007 (Frient Guidance Paper Transitional Justice), in: http://www.frient.de/downloads/FriEnt_Guidance%20Paper%20Transitional%20Justice_2007.pdf (12.01.2008).

Edited Books

American Psychological Association (ed.): Forgiveness. A Sampling of Research Results (Compiled by the American Psychological Association on the Occasion of the 59th Annual DPI/NGO Conference United Nations Headquarters, Midday Workshop "Forgiveness: Partnering with the Enemy"), Washington D.C. 2006, in: http://www.apa.org/international/un-forgive.pdf (12.01.2008).

Barbanel, Laura/Sternberg, Robert (eds.): Psychological Interventions in Times of Crisis, New York 2006.

Biggar, Nigel (ed.): Burying the Past. Making Peace and Doing Justice After Violent Conflict, Washington D.C. 2003.

Bloomfield, David/Barnes, Teresa/Huyse, Luc (eds.): Reconciliation After Violent Conflict. A Handbook, Stockholm 2003 (International Institute for Democracy and Electoral Assistance), in: http://www.idea.int/publications/reconciliation/upload/reconciliation_full.pdf (12.01.2008).

Bloomfield, David/Fischer, Martina/Schmelzle, Beatrix (eds.): Berghof Handbook for Conflict Transformation, Berlin 2004, in: http://www.berghof-handbook.net/std_page.php?LANG=e&id=11 (02.06.2008).

Calliess, Jörg (ed.): Zehn Jahre danach. Völkermord in Ruanda, Loccum 2005 (Dokumentation einer Tagung der evangelischen Akademie Loccum vom 5. bis 7. März 2004).

Chayes, Antonia/Minow, Martha (eds.): Imagine Coexistence. Restoring Humanity after Violent Ethnic Conflict, San Francisco et al. 2003.

Guichaoua, André (ed.): Les Crises Politiques au Burundi et au Rwanda (1993-1994). Analyses, Faits et Documents, 2nd edition, Paris 1995.

Harding, Leonard (ed.): Ruanda – der Weg zum Völkermord. Vorgeschichte, Verlauf, Deutung, Hamburg 1998.

Jokie, Alexsandar (ed.): War Crimes and Collective Wrongdoing, Oxford 2001.

Mayor, Federico/Matoko, Edouard (eds.): Les fondements endogènes d'une culture de la paix en Afrique. Mécanismes traditionnels de prévention et de résolution des conflits, Paris 1999 (United Nations Educational, Scientific and Cultural Organization Publication), in: http://www.unesco.org/cpp/publications/mecanismes (12.06.2008).

Starken, Brian (ed.): Working for Reconciliation. A Caritas Handbook, Vatican City 1999, in: http://www.caritas.org/static/pdf/eng/wkgreconc.pdf (12.01.2008).

Stover, Eric et al. (eds.): My Neighbour, My Enemy. Justice and Community in the Aftermath of Mass Atrocity, Cambridge 2004.

Woyke, Wichard (ed.): Handwörterbuch Internationale Politik, 8th updated edition, Bonn 2000 (Schriftenreihe Bundeszentrale für politische Bildung Band 404).

Articles in Edited Books

Afzali, Aneelah/Colleton, Laura: Constructing Coexistence. A Survey of Coexistence Projects in Areas of Ethnic Conflict, in: Chayes, Antonia/Minow, Martha (eds.): Imagine Coexistence. Restoring Humanity after Violent Ethnic Conflict, San Francisco et al. 2003, pp. 3-20.

Bah, Thierno: Les Mécanismes traditionnels de prévention et de résolution des conflits en Afrique noire, in: Mayor, Federico/Matoko, Edouard (eds.): Les fondements endogènes d'une culture de la paix en Afrique. Mécanismes traditionnels de prévention et de résolution des conflits, Paris 1999 (United Nations Educational, Scientific and Cultural Organization Publication), in: http://www.unesco.org/cpp/publications/mecanismes/edbah.htm (12.06.2008).

Biggar, Nigel: Making Peace or Doing Justice. Must We Choose?, in: Biggar, Nigel (ed.): Burying the Past. Making Peace and Doing Justice After Violent Conflict, Washington D.C. 2003, pp. 3-24.

Bloomfield, David: Reconciliation. An Introduction, in: Bloomfield, David/Barnes, Teresa/Huyse, Luc (eds.): Reconciliation After Violent Conflict. A Handbook, Stockholm 2003 (International Institute for Democracy and Electoral Assistance), pp. 10-18, in: http://www.idea.int/publications/reconciliation/upload/reconciliation_full.pdf (12.01.2008).

Bloomfield, David: The Context of Reconciliation, in: Bloomfield, David/Barnes, Teresa/Huyse, Luc (eds.): Reconciliation After Violent Conflict. A Handbook, Stockholm 2003 (International Institute for Democracy and Electoral Assistance), pp. 40-48, in: http://www.idea.int/publications/reconciliation/upload/reconciliation_full.pdf (12.01.2008).

Boege, Volker: Traditional Approaches to Conflict Transformation. Potentials and Limits, in: Bloomfield, David/Fischer, Martina/Schmelzle, Beatrix (eds.): Berghof Handbook for Conflict Transformation, Berlin 2004, pp. 1-21, in: http://www.berghof-handbook.net/uploads/download/boege_handbook.pdf (02.06.2008).

Burns, Cynthia/McGrew, Laura/Todorovic, Ilija: Imagine Coexistence Pilot Projects in Rwanda and Bosnia, in: Chayes, Antonia/Minow, Martha (eds.): Imagine Coexistence. Restoring Humanity after Violent Ethnic Conflict, San Francisco et al. 2003, pp. 85-101.

Chayes, Antonia/Minow, Martha: Introduction, in: Chayes, Antonia/Minow, Martha (eds.): Imagine Coexistence. Restoring Humanity after Violent Ethnic Conflict, San Francisco et al. 2003, pp. xvii – xxii.

Crocker, David A.: Transitional Justice and International Civil Society, in: Jokie, Alexsandar (ed.): War Crimes and Collective Wrongdoing, Oxford 2001, pp. 270-300.

Elshtain, Jean Bethke: Politics and Forgiveness, in: Biggar, Nigel (ed.): Burying the Past. Making Peace and Doing Justice After Violent Conflict, Washington D.C. 2003, pp. 45-64.

Forsberg, Tuomas: The Philosophy and Practice of Dealing With the Past. Some Conceptual and Normative Issues, in: Biggar, Nigel (ed.): Burying the Past. Making Peace and Doing Justice After Violent Conflict, Washington D.C. 2003, pp. 65-84.

Guichaoua, André: La région des Grands Lacs. Un lourd passé, un présent dramatique, un avenir des plus sombres, in: Guichaoua, André (ed.): Les Crises Politiques au Burundi et au Rwanda (1993-1994). Analyses, Faits et Documents, 2nd edition, Paris 1995, pp. 19-51.

Hamber, Brandon: Does the Truth Heal? A Psychological Perspective on Political Strategies for Dealing With the Legacy of Political Violence, in: Biggar, Nigel (ed.): Burying the Past. Making Peace and Doing Justice After Violent Conflict, Washington D.C. 2003, pp. 155-174.

Hamber, Brandon: Healing, in: Bloomfield, David/Barnes, Teresa/Huyse, Luc (eds.): Reconciliation After Violent Conflict. A Handbook, Stockholm 2003 (International Institute for Democracy and Electoral Assistance), pp. 77-88, in: http://www.idea.int/publications/reconciliation/upload/reconciliation_full.pdf (12.01.2008).

Hankel, Gerd: Über den schwierigen Versuch der Vergangenheitsaufarbeitung in Ruanda, in: Calliess, Jörg (ed.): Zehn Jahre danach. Völkermord in Ruanda, Loccum 2005

(Dokumentation einer Tagung der evangelischen Akademie Loccum vom 5. bis 7. März 2004), pp. 105-111.

Harding, Leonard/Heeger, Carsten: Versuch einer Erklärung. Eine theoretische Annäherung an den Völkermord, in: Harding, Leonard (ed.): Ruanda – der Weg zum Völkermord. Vorgeschichte, Verlauf, Deutung, Hamburg 1998, pp. 207-221.

Heeger, Carsten: Die Erfindung der Ethnien in der Kolonialzeit. „Am Anfang stand das Wort", in: Harding, Leonard (ed.): Ruanda – der Weg zum Völkermord. Vorgeschichte, Verlauf, Deutung, Hamburg 1998, pp. 21-35.

Hufmann, Matthias: Die Verunsicherung von außen und der Aufbau eines neuen Feindbildes, in: Harding, Leonard (ed.): Ruanda – der Weg zum Völkermord. Vorgeschichte, Verlauf, Deutung, Hamburg 1998, pp. 99-109.

Huyse, Luc: The Process of Reconciliation, in: Bloomfield, David/Barnes, Teresa/Huyse, Luc (eds.): Reconciliation After Violent Conflict. A Handbook, Stockholm 2003 (International Institute for Democracy and Electoral Assistance), pp. 19-33, in: http://www.idea.int/publications/reconciliation/upload/reconciliation_full.pdf (12.01.2008).

Huyse, Luc: Victims, in: Bloomfield, David/Barnes, Teresa/Huyse, Luc (eds.): Reconciliation After Violent Conflict. A Handbook, Stockholm 2003 (International Institute for Democracy and Electoral Assistance), pp. 54-66, in:

http://www.idea.int/publications/reconciliation/upload/reconciliation_full.pdf (12.01.2008).

Huyse, Luc: Justice, in: Bloomfield, David/Barnes, Teresa/Huyse, Luc (eds.): Reconciliation After Violent Conflict. A Handbook, Stockholm 2003 (International Institute for Democracy and Electoral Assistance), pp. 97-114, in: http://www.idea.int/publications/reconciliation/upload/reconciliation_full.pdf (12.01.2008).

Longman, Timothy/Rutagengwa, Théonèste: Memory, Identity and Community in Rwanda, in: Stover, Eric et al. (eds.): My Neighbour, My Enemy. Justice and Community in the Aftermath of Mass Atrocity, Cambridge 2004, pp. 162-182.

Longman, Timothy/Pham, Phuong/Weinstein, Harvey: Connecting Justice to Human Experience. Attitudes Towards Accountability and Reconciliation in Rwanda, in: Stover, Eric et al. (eds.): My Neighbour, My Enemy. Justice and Community in the Aftermath of Mass Atrocity, Cambridge 2004, pp. 207-225.

Nsengiyaremye, Joel: Zehn Jahre danach. Völkermord in Ruanda, in: Calliess, Jörg (ed.): Zehn Jahre danach. Völkermord in Ruanda, Loccum 2005 (Dokumentation einer Tagung der evangelischen Akademie Loccum vom 5. bis 7. März 2004), pp. 91-96.

Philpot, Catherine/Hornsey, Matthew: Asking Forgiveness for the Sins of Many. Does it Work?, in: American Psychological Association (ed.): Forgiveness. A Sampling of Research

Results (Compiled by the American Psychological Association on the Occasion of the 59th Annual DPI/NGO Conference United Nations Headquarters, Midday Workshop "Forgiveness: Partnering with the Enemy"), Washington 2006, pp. 22-24, in: http://www.apa.org/international/un-forgive.pdf (12.01.2008).

Reinhardt, Wolfgang: Signs of Hope After the Genocide. Healing and Reconciliation in Rwanda Today, in: Calliess, Jörg (ed.): Zehn Jahre danach. Völkermord in Ruanda, Loccum 2005 (Dokumentation einer Tagung der evangelischen Akademie Loccum vom 5. bis 7. März 2004), pp. 187-204.

Rink, Eva/Schreiber, Wolfgang: Die Entdeckung von Ethnizität und die Bildung politischer Parteien, in: Harding, Leonard (ed.): Ruanda – der Weg zum Völkermord. Vorgeschichte, Verlauf, Deutung, Hamburg 1998, pp. 37-56.

Shriver, Donald W.: Where and When in Political Life Is Justice Served by Forgiveness?, in: Biggar, Nigel (ed.): Burying the Past. Making Peace and Doing Justice After Violent Conflict, Washington D.C. 2003, pp. 25-43.

Siebels, Stefan: Die Flüchtlingskrise, in: Harding, Leonard (ed.): Ruanda – der Weg zum Völkermord. Vorgeschichte, Verlauf, Deutung, Hamburg 1998, pp. 183-194.

Sluzki, Carlos E.: The Process Toward Reconciliation, in: Chayes, Antonia/Minow, Martha (eds.): Imagine Coexistence. Restoring Humanity after Violent Ethnic Conflict, San Francisco et al. 2003, pp. 21-31.

Sommers, Marc/McClintock, Elizabeth: On Hidden Ground. One Coexistence Strategy in Central Africa, in: Chayes, Antonia/Minow, Martha (eds.): Imagine Coexistence. Restoring Humanity after Violent Ethnic Conflict, San Francisco et al. 2003, pp. 35-58.

Spelman, Elizabeth V.: Coexistence and Repair, in: Chayes, Antonia/Minow, Martha (eds.): Imagine Coexistence. Restoring Humanity after Violent Ethnic Conflict, San Francisco et al. 2003, pp. 235-250.

Spengemann, Sven M.: Freedom's Hidden Price. Framing the Obstacles to Economic Coexistence, in: Chayes, Antonia/Minow, Martha (eds.): Imagine Coexistence. Restoring Humanity after Violent Ethnic Conflict, San Francisco et al. 2003, pp. 131-151.

Staub, Ervin/Pearlman, Laurie Anne: Advancing Healing and Reconciliation, in: Barbanel, Laura/Sternberg, Robert (eds.): Psychological Interventions in Times of Crisis, New York 2006, pp. 213-243.

Staub, Ervin/Pearlman, Laurie Anne: Promoting Reconciliation and Forgiveness After Mass Violence. Rwanda and Other Settings, in: American Psychological Association (ed.): Forgiveness. A Sampling of Research Results (Compiled by the American Psychological Association on the Occasion of the 59th Annual DPI/NGO Conference United Nations Headquarters, Midday Workshop "Forgiveness: Partnering with the Enemy"), Washington 2006, pp. 24-26, in: http://www.apa.org/international/un-forgive.pdf (12.01.2008).

Theissen, Gunnar: Supporting Justice, Coexistence and Reconciliation After Armed Conflict. Strategies for Dealing with the Past, in: Bloomfield, David/Fischer, Martina/Schmelzle, Beatrix (eds.): Berghof Handbook for Conflict Transformation, Berlin 2004, pp. 1-18, in: http://www.berghof-handbook.net/uploads/download/theissen_handbook.pdf (16.12.2007).

Trines, Stefan: Unterlassene Hilfeleistung bei Völkermord? Die UN und der Ruanda-Konflikt, in: Harding, Leonard (ed.): Ruanda – der Weg zum Völkermord. Vorgeschichte, Verlauf, Deutung, Hamburg 1998, pp. 159-169.

Tutu, Desmond: Foreword, in: Bloomfield, David/Barnes, Teresa/Huyse, Luc (eds.): Reconciliation After Violent Conflict. A Handbook, Stockholm 2003 (International Institute for Democracy and Electoral Assistance), p. 4, in: http://www.idea.int/publications/reconciliation/upload/reconciliation_full.pdf (12.01.2008).

Uvin, Peter: The Gacaca Tribunals in Rwanda, in: Bloomfield, David/Barnes, Teresa/Huyse, Luc (eds.): Reconciliation After Violent Conflict. A Handbook, Stockholm 2003 (International Institute for Democracy and Electoral Assistance), pp. 116-121, in: http://www.idea.int/publications/reconciliation/upload/reconciliation_full.pdf (12.01.2008).

Vandeginste, Stef: Rwanda. Dealing with Genocide and Crimes against Humanity in the Context of Armed Conflict and Failed Political Transition, in: Biggar, Nigel (ed.): Burying the

Past. Making Peace and Doing Justice After Violent Conflict, Washington D.C. 2003, pp. 251-285.

Wissbar, Katrin: Guter Hutu - Böser Tutsi. Der Aufstieg der Hutu Power, in: Harding, Leonard (ed.): Ruanda – der Weg zum Völkermord. Vorgeschichte, Verlauf, Deutung, Hamburg 1998, pp. 125-138.

Wohl, Michael J.A./Branscombe, Nyla R.: Forgiving the Ingroup or the Outgroup for Harm Doing, in: American Psychological Association (ed.): Forgiveness. A Sampling of Research Results (Compiled by the American Psychological Association on the Occasion of the 59th Annual DPI/NGO Conference United Nations Headquarters, Midday Workshop "Forgiveness: Partnering with the Enemy"), Washington 2006, pp. 18-20, in: http://www.apa.org/international/un-forgive.pdf (12.01.2008).

Magazine Articles

Amstutz, Mark R.: Is Reconciliation Possible After Genocide? The Case of Rwanda, in: Journal of Church and State, Vol. 48 (2006) 3, pp. 541-566.

Betts, Alexander: Should Approaches to Post-Conflict Justice and Reconciliation Be Determined Globally, Nationally or Locally?, in: The European Journal of Development Research, Vol. 17 (2005) 4, pp. 735-752.

Braeckmann, Colette: Rwanda. The Challenges After Victory, in: African Geopolitics, Vol. 13 (2004), in: http://www.african-geopolitics.org/home_english.htm (12.01.2008).

Cobban, Helena: The Legacies of Collective Violence. The Rwandan Genocide and the Limits of Law, in: The Boston Review, Vol. 27 (2002) 2, in: http://bostonreview.net/BR27.2/cobban.html (16.02.2008).

Cobban, Helena: Healing Rwanda. Can an International Court Deliver Justice ?, in: The Boston Review, Vol. 28 (2003) 5, in : http://bostonreview.net/BR28.6/cobban.html (16.02.2008).

Corey, Allison/Joireman, Sandra: Retributive Justice. The Gacaca Courts in Rwanda, in: African Affairs, Vol. 103 (2004) 1, pp. 73-89.

Daly, Erin: Between Punitive and Reconstructive Justice. The Gacaca Courts in Rwanda, in: Journal of International Law and Politics, Vol. 34 (2002) 2, pp. 355-396.

Drumbl, Mark Antonin: Punishment, Postgenocide. From Guilt to Shame to Civis in Rwanda, in: New York University Law Review, Vol. 75 (2000) 5, pp. 1221-1326.

Emizet, Kisangani N. F.: The Massacre of Refugees in Congo. A Case of UN Peacekeeping Failure and International Law, in: Journal of Modern African Studies, Vol. 28 (2000) 2, pp. 163-202.

Fisiy, Cyprian F.: Of Journeys and Border Crossings. Return of Refugees, Identity, and

Reconstruction in Rwanda, in: African Studies Review, Vol. 41 (1998) 1, pp. 17-28.

Fletcher, Laurel E./Weinstein, Harvey M.: Violence and Social Repair. Rethinking the Contribution of Justice to Reconciliation, in: Human Rights Quarterly, Vol. 24 (2002) 3, pp. 573-639.

Gobodo-Madikizela, Pumla: Trauma und Versöhnung. Lehren aus Südafrika, in: Aus Politik und Zeitgeschichte, (2006) 42, pp. 32-38.

Graybill, Lyn S.: Pardon, Punishment, and Amnesia. Three African Post-conflict Methods, in: Third World Quarterly, Vol. 25 (2004) 6, pp. 1117-1130.

Gready, Paul: Reconceptualising Transitional Justice. Embedded and Distanced Justice, in: Conflict, Security and Development, Vol. 5 (2005) 1, pp. 3-21.

Gubin, Alexander/Hagengimana, Athanase/Pearlman, Laurie Anne/Staub, Ervin: Healing, Reconciliation, Forgiving and the Prevention of Violence After Genocide or Mass Killing. An Intervention and its Experimental Evaluation in Rwanda, in: Journal of Social and Clinical Psychology, Vol. 24 (2005) 3, pp. 297-334.

Hankel, Gerd: Vergangenheit, die nicht ruhen darf. Essay, in: Aus Politik und Zeitgeschichte, (2006) 42, pp. 3-9.

Hornberger, Kusi: Rwandan Gacaca Courts in Crisis. Is There a Case for Judicial Review?, in: Africa Policy Journal, Vol. 3 (2007), pp. 1- 25, in:

http://www.hks.harvard.edu/kssgorg/apj/issues/spring_2007_issue/pdfs/Kusi.article.pdf (12.03.2008)

Khadiagala, Gilbert M./Lyons, Terrence: The Challenges of Leadership in Post-Conflict Transitions. Lessons from Africa, in: Conflict Trends, (2006) 4, pp. 9-15, in: http://www.accord.org.za/ct/2006-4/CT4_2006_pg9-15.pdf (15.03.2008).

Lemarchand, René: Genocide in the Great Lakes. Which Genocide? Whose Genocide?, in: African Studies Review, Vol. 41 (1998) 1, pp. 3-16.

Le Mon, Christopher J.: Rwanda's Troubled Gacaca Courts, in: Human Rights Brief, Vol. 14 (2007) 2, pp. 16-20, in: http://www.wcl.american.edu/hrbrief/14/2lemon.pdf?rd=1 (23.03.2008).

Mackintosh, Anne: Rwanda. Beyond Ethnic Conflict, in: Development in Practice, Vol. 7 (1997) 4, pp. 464-474.

Mamdani, Mahmood: From Conquest to Consent as the Basis of State Formation. Reflections on Rwanda, in: New Left Review, Vol. 216 (1996) 1, pp. 3-36.

Maogoto, Jackson Nyamuya: The International Criminal Tribunal for Rwanda. A Distorting Mirror. Casting Doubt on its Actor Oriented Approach in Addressing the Rwandan Genocide, in: African Journal on Conflict Resolution, Vol. 3 (2003) 1, pp. 55-97, in: http://www.accord.org.za/ajcr/2003-1/accordr_v3_n1_a8.pdf (16.12.2007).

McNairn, Rosemarie: Building Capacity to Resolve Conflict in Communities. Oxfam Experience in Rwanda, in: Gender and Development, Vol. 12 (2004) 3, pp. 83-93.

Mgbako, Chi: Ingando Solidarity Camps. Reconciliation and Political Indoctrination in Post-Genocide Rwanda, in: Harvard Human Rights Journal, Vol. 18 (2005), pp. 201-224, in: http://www.law.harvard.edu/students/orgs/hrj/iss18/mgbako.pdf (23.03.2008).

Mthembu-Salter, Gregory: Mediation and Genocide in Rwanda and Burundi's Peace Agreement Without Peace, in: Track Two, Vol. 11 (2002) 5/6, in: http://ccrweb.ccr.uct.ac.za/archive/two/11_56/rwanda_chapter2.html (16.12.2007).

Oomen, Barbara: Donor-Driven Justice and its Discontents. The Case of Rwanda, in: Development and Change, Vol. 36 (2005) 5, pp. 887-910.

Pankhurst, Donna: Issues of Justice and Reconciliation in Complex Political Emergencies. Conceptualising Reconciliation, Justice and Peace, in: Third World Quarterly, Vol. 20 (1999) 1, pp. 239-256.

Reyntjens, Filip: Le Gacaca ou la Justice du Gazon au Rwanda, in: Politique Africaine, Vol. 40 (1990), pp. 31-41, in: http://www.politique-africaine.com/numeros/pdf/040031.pdf (11.02.2008).

Reynjens, Filip: Rwanda, Ten Years On. From Genocide to Dictatorship, in: African Affairs, Vol. 103 (2004) 411, pp. 177-210.

Reyntjens, Filip: Post-1994 Politics in Rwanda. Problematising "Liberation" and "Democratisation", in: Third World Quarterly, Vol. 27 (2006) 6, pp. 1103-1117.

Richters, Annemiek/Dekker, Cora/De Jonge, Klaas: Reconciliation in the Aftermath of Violent Conflict in Rwanda, in: Intervention, Vol. 3 (2005) 3, pp. 203-221.

Sandbrook, Richard: Transitions Without Consolidation. Democratization in Six African Cases, in: Third World Quarterly, Vol. 17 (1996) 1, pp. 69-88.

Sarkin, Jeremy: The Necessity and Challenges of Establishing a Truth and Reconciliation Commission in Rwanda, in: Human Rights Quarterly, Vol. 21 (1999) 3, pp. 776-823.

Sarkin, Jeremy: The Tension Between Justice and Reconciliation in Rwanda. Politics, Human Rights, Due Process and the Role of the Gacaca Courts in Dealing With the Genocide, in: Journal of African Law, Vol. 45 (2001) 2, pp. 143-172.

Sidiropoulos, Elizabeth: Democratisation and Militarisation in Rwanda. Eight Years After the Genocide, in: African Security Review, Vol. 11 (2002) 3, in: http://www.iss.co.za/ASR/11No3/Sidiropoulos.html (10.01.2008).

Smith, Joshua G.: Fighting Fear. Exploring the Dynamic Between Security Concerns and Elite Manipulation in Internal Conflict, in: Peace, Conflict and Development, Vol. 8 (2006) 8, pp. 1-32, in: http://www.peacestudiesjournal.org.uk/docs/Feb%2006%20SMITH.pdf (15.03.2008).

Spears, Ian S.: Understanding Inclusive Peace Agreements in Africa. The Problems of Sharing Power, in: Third World Quarterly, Vol. 21 (2000) 1, pp. 105-118.

Tiemessen, Alana Erin: After Arusha. Gacaca Justice in Post-Genocide Rwanda, in: African Studies Quarterly, Vol. 8 (2004) 1, pp. 57-76.

Uvin, Peter: Reading the Rwandan Genocide, in: International Studies Review, Vol. 3 (2001) 3, pp. 75-99.

Uvin, Peter/Mironko, Charles: Western and Local Approaches to Justice in Rwanda, in: Global Governance, Vol. 9 (2003), pp. 219-231.

Wagner, Andreas: Mauern des Schweigens brechen. Gegenseitiges Verständnis fördert den ruandischen Versöhnungsprozess, in: DED Brief, Vol. 44 (2007) 4, pp. 27-29.

Wegemund, Regina: Nationale Aussöhnung in Ruanda. Chancen und Bedrohung, in: Internationales Afrikaforum, Vol. 38 (2002) 4, pp. 363-373.

Wenke, Daja: Gacaca Rechtssprechung in Ruanda. Ein traditionelles Gerichtsverfahren in modernisierter Form. Struktur, Probleme und Chancen, in: Stichproben. Wiener Zeitschrift für kritische Afrikastudien, Vol. 2 (2002) 4, pp. 23-54.

Werchick, Leah: Prospects for Justice in Rwanda's Citizen Tribunals, in: Human Rights Brief, Vol. 8 (2002) 3, in: http://www.wcl.american.edu/hrbrief/08/3rwanda.cfm (12.06.2008).

Wierzynska, Aneta: Consolidating Democracy Through Rwanda's Transitional Gacaca Courts, in: New York University Law Review, Vol. 79 (2004) 5, pp. 1934-1969, in: http://www.law.nyu.edu/JOURNALS/LAWREVIEW/issues/vol79/no5/NYU508.pdf (15.03.2008).

Zorbas, Eugenia: Reconciliation in Post-genocide Rwanda, in: African Journal of Legal Studies, Vol. 1 (2004) 1, pp. 29-52.

Newspaper Articles

Molt, Peter: Eine gewaltsame "Lösung" der Flüchtlingsfrage, in: FAZ (02.11.1996), p. 8.

Rwanda. Traditional Courts inaugurated, in: IRIN News (24.06.2004), in: http://www.irinnews.org/report.aspx?reportid=50380 (30.06.2008).

Walker, Robert: Genocide Hatred Lingers in Rwanda Schools, in: BBC News (19.02.2008), in: http://news.bbc.co.uk/go/pr/fr/-/2/hi/africa/7246985.stm (19.02.2008).

Walker, Robert: Rwandan Jail for Genocide Guilty (04.03.2008), in: BBC News, in: http://news.bbc.co.uk/go/pr/fr/-/2/hi/africa/7277995.stm (10.3.2008).

Walker, Robert: Rwandans Still Divided 10 Years On (07.04.2004), in: BBC News, in: http://news.bbc.co.uk/go/pr/fr/-/2/hi/africa/3557565.stm (29.01.2008).

Walker, Robert: Rwanda "Still Teaching Genocide" (17.01.2008), in: BBC News, in: http://news.bbc.co.uk/go/pr/fr/-/2/hi/africa/7194827.stm (18.01.2008).

Walker, Robert: Rwanda Anger at Genocide Tribunal (30.05.2008), in: BBC News, in: http://news.bbc.co.uk/2/hi/africa/7427249.stm (01.06.2008).

Walker, Robert: Rwanda Still Searching for Justice (04.03.2008), in: BBC News, in: http://news.bbc.co.uk/2/hi/africa/3557753.stm (14.06.2008).

8 Abbreviations

BBC: British Broadcasting Cooperation
DED/ZFD: Deutscher Entwicklungsdienst/Ziviler Friedensdienst
DRC: Democratic Republic of the Congo
FES: Friedrich Ebert Stiftung
G.P.: Garde Presidentielle
GTZ: Gesellschaft für technische Zusammenarbeit
HIV: Human Immunodeficiency Virus
ICC: International Criminal Court
IDEA: International Institute for Democracy and Electoral Assistance
ICTR: International Criminal Tribunal for Rwanda
MDR: Mouvement Démocratique Républicain (Democratic Republican Movement)
MRND: Mouvement Revolutionaire Nationale Pour le Developpement (National Revolutionary Movement for Development)
NGO: Non-Governmental Organization
NURC: National Unity and Reconciliation Commission
ODA: Official Development Aid
PRI: Penal Reform International
PTSD: Post-Traumatic Stress Disorder
RPA: Rwandan Patriotic Army
RPF: Rwandan Patriotic Front
SIDA: Swedish International Development Agency
TRC: South African Truth and Reconciliation Commission
TPIR: Tribunal Pénal International Pour Le Rwanda
UN: United Nations
UNDP: United Nations Development Programme
UNESCO: United Nations Educational, Scientific and Cultural Organization
USD: United States Dollar

In der Schriftenreihe *Bonner Studien zum globalen Wandel* sind bisher erschienen:

Nina Hürter:
Is a mission shared a problem halved?
Grenzen und Perspektiven regionaler
Friedensmissionen im Auftrag der
Vereinten Nationen
(Band 1)
152 Seiten, 24,90 Euro, 2009
ISBN 978-3-8288-2125-5